Tools of the Spirit

Tools of the Spirit

Pathways to the Realization of Universal Innocence

by

Robert Dilts

and

Robert McDonald

Meta Publications Inc.
P.O. Box 1910, Capitola, CA 95010
(831) 464-0254 Fax (831) 464-0517
E-Mail: metapub@prodigy.net
Website: www.meta-publications.com

Library of Congress Card Number 97-072115
I.S.B.N. 0-916990-40-0

Contents

Dedication   ix

Acknowledgments   xi

INTRODUCTION   xiii

  Birth, Death and Rebirth   xiv

  Integrity   xv

PART ONE: **BIRTH**

CHAPTER 1   WHAT IS 'TOOLS OF THE SPIRIT?'   3

  The Wise Rabbi   5

  Silence   6

  What It's All About   6

  "And Then a Miracle Happens"   7

  The Two Lines Into Heaven   10

  Emphasis on Experience   10

  Small "s" and Large "S" Self   11

  A Dream of the Large "S" Self   12

  Uniting the Small "s" and Large "S" Selves   14

  Fear, Love and Forgiveness   15

CHAPTER 2   CO-ALIGNMENT   17

  Levels of Experience   18

  An Analogy to the Roots and Branches

    of a Tree   21

  "Neuro-Logical" Levels   22

  Level Co-Alignment   24

  Summary of Logical Level Co-Alignment

    Process   35

CHAPTER 3   SACRED JOURNEY   37
  Sacred Journey   38
  An Image of the Large "S" Self   43
  Introductions Using Drawings of
    the Large "S" Self   44
  Map and Territory   46

CHAPTER 4   PRESENCE OF ETERNITY   47
  Presence of Eternity   48
  Time Lines and "Anchoring"   48
  "Whenever Two or More Are Gathered
    in My Name"   51
  The Presence of Eternity Process   52
  Summary of the Presence of Eternity –
    Integrating Time Frames   58

CHAPTER 5   SPIRITUAL HEALING   59
  Mercy and Forgiveness   60
  The Story of the King and Queen   60
  Unmerited Mercy   62
  Healing Relationships   65
  Perceptual Positions   66
  The Spiritual Healing Process   68
  Summary of the Spiritual Healing Process   80
  Basic Elements of Healing   83

PART TWO: DEATH

CHAPTER 6   OPENING TO THE SHADOW   87
  Letting Go of the Unnecessary   88
  What Do You Want?   88
  Changing in the Twinkling of an Eye   89
  Meaningful and Meaningless Pain   92
  Robert Dilts' Daughter:
    Shadows and Light   101

Robert McDonald's Father:
  Loving Anyway   103
Opening to the Shadow   107
Forms of Enmeshment   111
Discovering the Shadow   112

CHAPTER 7   RELEASING ENMESHMENT
             WITH THE SHADOW   113
Robert Dilts' Shadow Work   114
  Exploring the Structure of the Shadow   114
  Finding the Positive Purpose of the
    Shadow Attachment   116
  Sculpting a 'Spiritually Evolving' Self   118
  Discovering the 'Spiritually Evolving'
    Essence of the Shadow   119
  Checking for Objections to Releasing
    the Shadow   120
  Releasing the Connection with the Shadow   121
  Attaching the Shadow to Its
    'Spiritually Evolving Essence'   121
  Connecting with the 'Spiritually
    Evolving' Self   122
  Stabilizing the Transformation   123
Summary of the Releasing Enmeshment
  with the Shadow Process   126
Discussion of the Releasing Enmeshment
  Process   129
  Handling Possible Objections   131
Releasing Enmeshment as a Path
  to Spiritual Growth   133
Robert McDonald's Shadow Work   134
The Emperor's Looking Glass   135
Saying Good-Bye   137
The Monk and the Tiger   139

CHAPTER 8   SELF PARENTING   141
  My Friend John and the Tiger   142
  Forgive and Remember   144
    'Imprinting' and the Self Parenting Process   146
  The Self Parenting Process   148
    Finding the Symbol of the Mother   148
    Finding the Symbol of the Father   149
    Finding the Gift of the Mother   151
    Finding the Gift of the Father   152
    Helping the Mother Understand the
      Gift of the Father   153
    Helping the Father Understand the
      Gift of the Mother   154
    Integrating the Mother and the Father   154
    Finding the Gift of the New Integration of
      the Mother and Father   156
    Spreading the Gift of the Integration   156
  Summary of the Self Parenting Process   160

PART THREE: REBIRTH

CHAPTER 9   SYMBOLIC REBIRTH CYCLE   165
  Rebirth   166
  Silly Greetings   166
  Stories: A Tool to Celebrate Rebirth   168
  Mary and Joseph on Their Way to Bethlehem   168
  Cycles of Change   169
  Storytelling   174
  The Symbolic Rebirth Cycle (The Never
    Ending Story)   175
  Symbolic Rebirth Worksheet   177
  Creating your Symbols   179
    Yearning for Spiritual Wholeness   179
    Your Large "S" Self   180
    Opening to Spiritual Awakening   181

Currently Embodying - The Small "s" Self   182
The Shadow   183
Opening to Letting Go of the Unnecessary   184
Honoring the Shadow's Proper Place -
    The Museum of Personal History   185
Sacred Space   187
Telling Your Story   189
Robert Dilts' Story   192
Robert McDonald's Story   195
Those Who have Ears to Hear   198

CHAPTER 10 SPIRITUAL RENEWAL   199
Life Landscapes   200
Getting New Perspectives on Your Life   205
Generative Change   206
Spiritual Renewal: Tending Your Garden   207
Demonstration of the Spiritual
    Renewal Process   208
    1st Position Present - Present Self   208
    1st Position Future - Future Self   209
    2nd Position Future - Future Other   211
    3rd Position Future - Future Observer   213
    2nd Position Present - Present Other   214
    3rd Position Present - Present Observer   215
    1st Position Past - Past Self   216
    2nd Position Past - Past Other   218
    3rd Position Past - Past Observer   220
    Pat's Metaphor   222
    Practicing the Spiritual Renewal Process   224
Steps of the Spiritual Renewal Process   225

CHAPTER 11 CLOSING   231
Final Drawings of the Large 'S' Self   232
Readings   233
Is the Universe a Friendly Place?   235

APPENDIX A: INSPIRATIONAL READINGS   237
  Presuppositions of NLP   239
  An Emotional and Spiritual Vocabulary   242
  On Defining the Spirit   244
  The Finite and The Infinite   246
  Summary of the Perennial Philosophy   247
  Embracing the Vision of NLP   252
  Amazing Grace   257
  Readings   258

APPENDIX B: THE PRINCIPLE OF
  POSITIVE INTENTION   265

APPENDIX C: SPIRITUAL REUNION –
  DEALING WITH SEPARATION, LOSS AND GRIEF   277

BIBLIOGRAPHY   279

INDEX   281

AFTERWORD   289

Dedication

To the Spirit of all those who
continue to expand our awareness
of universal innocence.

Acknowledgments

We would like to acknowledge:

Gregory Bateson for his wisdom about the "larger mind" in which we participate and his contributions to the concept of logical levels.

Richard Bandler and John Grinder for sparking the light of NLP and revealing "the vast darkness of the subject."

Ken Wilber for his extraordinarily explicit discussions of the non-dual and ineffable nature of the Spirit.

Steve and Connirae Andreas for contributing so much to help ground and simplify the concepts of NLP, specifically as a therapeutic tool.

Thaddeus Golas for his *Lazy Man's Guide to Enlightenment*.

Tom Dotz for sponsoring the first *Tools of the Spirit* program, and all of the other institutes and individuals who have graciously supported our *Tools of the Spirit* seminars around the world.

Our families who have travelled with us on our spiritual journey through life, creating the context for us to naturally discover our own authenticity, humility and grace.

Introduction

Tools of the Spirit is a book about understanding and strengthening our relationship to the larger systems of which we are a part. The material covered in this book began as a seminar to explore the ways in which the models and tools of Neuro-Linguistic Programming (NLP) could contribute to creating a greater sense of what people call "spiritual connection" and "wholeness."

We believe that the mission of NLP is to "create a world to which people want to belong." In *Tools of the Spirit* we seek to contribute to this mission by providing skills for living in a state of what Castenada's don Juan called *"impeccability"*. For us, impeccability is a state of authenticity, humility and grace, guided by the awareness of change, impermanence and the immediacy of death.

Authenticity comes from being associated in your own body and being congruent about your own experience. *Humility* involves knowing your limits, appreciating the intentions, strengths and perspectives of others. *Grace* is unmerited mercy, which results from perceiving the world with impartial love. In a state of grace a person experiences a sense of full participation without self-judgment or arrogance.

According to Aldous Huxley, the central problem for humanity is the quest for grace. And as Gregory Bateson pointed out, "For the attainment of grace, the reasons of the heart must be integrated with the reasons of the reason."

Integrating "heart" and "sword" – compassion and technology – is largely what *Tools of the Spirit* is about. NLP can be thought of as something that is essentially void of authenticity, humility and grace. It simply a tool, like a knife. You can use a knife to cut bread and serve your neighbor, or you can use the same knife to stab your neighbor. The knife has no heart and no vision. But the <u>person</u> who uses the knife, like the person who uses NLP, can bring heart, vision, compassion, understanding and love to the use of the tool. Our goal with *Tools of the Spirit* is to unite the tools which come from NLP with the heart, compassion and love which come from the "spirit" to create something new, illuminating, and powerful.

Historically, NLP has been about achieving tangible, concrete and observable objectives. We seek to apply NLP skills and techniques in the service of a broader vision. In fact, the meta-theme of *Tools of the Spirit* is "meaning." To us, "spirit" provides meaning for pain and hurt, as well as joy, celebration and love. We believe that if *Tools of the Spirit* does not in some way seek the meaning and transformation of individual and world suffering (such as the attempts at genocide that have occurred in places like Bosnia and Rwanda), if it does not address poverty, hatred, jealousy, and the human agony occuring in so many countries (including the USA), where people kill one another because one person has different religious beliefs or a different racial heritage than another, then it is just 'pie in the sky'. Our goal is to bring the healing awareness of universal innocence 'down to earth'.

Birth, Death and Rebirth

The *Tools of the Spirit* program is structured around three fundamental "archetypic" themes: birth, death and rebirth. These common life themes are often associated with the experience of the spiritual. The awareness of being part of something larger than ourselves typically occurs at times of birth and death, and produces the experience of rebirth. One of the primary reasons for rituals and ceremonies throughout the world is to mark out, physically, emotionally, intellectually, socially and spiritually, the personal and interpersonal transformations that happen at these times.

We have followed a similar pattern with this book. Part I is about birth – new beginnings. Part II is about death – 'letting go of that which is no longer necessary'. And Part III is about rebirth – reawakening to spiritual wholeness.

Integrity

The majority of this book has been drawn from a transcript of one of our *Tools of the Spirit* seminars. In pointing this out, it is important for us to add that we do not typically audiotape the *Tools of the Spirit* program. The primary reason is because we want to create an emotionally safe context such that people can open to themselves and others on a very deep level. This is more difficult to do if people are concerned about whether or not they are being recorded. Another reason is that our emphasis is on experience rather than information. Recording is often a 'meta message' that the information being presented is more important than our personal experience of it.

Gregory Bateson used to tell an interesting story about this issue. In the nineteen sixties, there was a lot of controversy and publicity relating to hallucinogenic drugs, such as LSD, marijuana, peyote, etc. During this time, the U.S. government outlawed the possession and use of many of these types of drugs. An issue arose regarding certain Native American groups who had been using peyote as part of their religious rituals for centuries. An anthropologist, named Sol Tax, who was studying one of these groups, knew that these Native Americans were not using drugs superficially. Peyote was a part of their religious practice and spiritual life. He realized that it would be devastating to their culture to make their rituals illegal. He devised a plan to make a videotape of the ritual and show it to the committee who intended to ban their use of peyote. He wanted the committee to see that this was a serious religious ceremony.

When Sol Tax presented his plan to the elders of the village of the tribe, all of them listened respectfully and agreed that it would be devastating to their culture and to their religious practice if the government prevented them from using this integral part of their ceremony. And they all agreed that it would probably be a good idea if the anthropologist videotaped the ceremony and showed it to the committee. Each in turn, however, excused himself from participating in the event if it were to be videotaped. At a certain point, Sol Tax began to realize that none of them were going to be in the ritual. He wouldn't be able to make the tape. He eventually realized that they were choosing their integrity over their survival. In their map of the world, it would have 'profaned' the ceremony to make a videotape of it. The purpose of the ceremony was to create an experience of intimacy and integrity. To record such an experience and show it for some other purpose would be to violate the very intention for which it was created. That would be as devastating a consequence as having lost their right to use peyote.

Similarly, we have felt that taping our *Tools of the Spirit* programs would somehow threaten the integrity of the experience for our participants.

However, due to the high demand for some kind of record or description of the seminar, we decided to take the risk of taping one seminar and having it transcribed. In order to preserve the privacy and intimacy of those who attended the program, we have deleted most of our interactions with the group, making this book essentially a conversation between Robert Dilts and Robert McDonald.

It is our hope and our intention to present *Tools of the Spirit* with authenticity, humility and grace. We hope you will receive it in the same spirit.

part one

Birth

What is 'Tools of the Spirit'?

Co-Alignment

Sacred Journey

Presence of Eternity

Spiritual Healing

Chapter 1

What is 'Tools of the Spirit'?

Overview of Chapter 1

- **The Wise Rabbi**
- **Silence**
- **What It's All About**
- **"And Then a Miracle Happens"**
- **The Two Lines Into Heaven**
- **Emphasis on Experience**
- **Small "s" and Large "S" Self**
- **A Dream of the Large "S" Self**
- **Uniting the Large "S" and Small "s" Selves**
- **Fear, Love and Forgiveness**

What is 'Tools of the Spirit'?

"I want to know how God created this world. I am not interested in this or that phenomenon, in the spectrum of this or that element; I want to know his thoughts; the rest are details."

- Albert Einstein

The term *Spirit*, as we will be using it in this book, may be likened to what Einstein was referring to as "God's thoughts." In the words of Gregory Bateson, Spirit is "the pattern which connects" all things together as a kind of "larger Mind" of which we as individuals are a subsystem.

Manifestations of this Spirit, in the form of wisdom, vision, mission and healing, are the results of acknowledging and bringing Spirit more into our lives and actions.

Fruits of the Spirit — such as love, compassion, joy and peace — are the generative and transformative results of being more in harmony with 'God's thoughts'; i.e., the patterns of this 'larger Mind'.

As human beings, the primary way we have of perceiving and embodying Spirit is through our nervous systems, our language and our mental maps or programs (our 'neuro-linguistic programs'). "Tools of the Spirit" are aids which bring our individual minds and nervous systems more in harmony and alignment with the 'larger Mind' and 'larger nervous system' of which we are members. Traditional 'tools of the Spirit' include such things as prayer, meditation, singing, dancing, parables, rituals, and blessings.

NLP can be considered a kind of 'meta tool' - a tool that can create other tools of the Spirit. The vision to be explored in this book is that of using NLP to 'create a world to which people want to belong' via developing skills for living in a state of *impeccability*. Impeccability is a state of authenticity, humility and grace guided by the awareness of change, impermanence and death.

NLP Tools — such as sensory awareness, multiple perspectives, neuro-logical levels, metaphor, anchoring and time lines — can be combined with the principle of 'positive intent' and the core presuppositions of NLP to create new and effective 'tools of the Spirit.' These tools can allow us to bring more of the manifestations and fruits of the Spirit into our lives and to connect and participate more fully and ecologically with the larger Mind and systems of which we are a part.

As you begin to read this book and do the exercises described within these pages, it will be important to keep these frames in mind.

The Wise Rabbi

There is a nice story about a famous Jewish Rabbi that illustrates some important aspects of our approach to Tools of the Spirit. This Rabbi was invited by the people of a small village to come and share his wisdom with them and teach them some of the secrets of the Torah. The villagers were in tremendous awe of the Rabbi and looked upon him with great reverence. On the evening of his talk the villagers filed silently into the meeting room, ready to receive his message with great seriousness. As the last villagers were entering the room, the Rabbi suddenly stood up and began to sing. He invited the group to sing with him and soon he broke into lively dance drawing the crowd along with him. Soon the room was filled with movement and laughter. As they finished the singing and dancing, all a bit surprised and out of breath, the Rabbi said, with a twinkle in his eye, "I trust that answers all your questions."

Silence

Robert Dilts: We like to start our *Tools of the Spirit* seminars with a few moments of silence and breathing. The purpose of this is to help people get the sense of being present. Perhaps you will join us.

Robert McDonald: If you have anything on your lap or in your hands you may want to put it on the floor. This is a time to let go of having to think about where your glasses are, or if your coffee cup is in the right place, or if your feet are in the right place. This is a time to come home to your body. Without the body we really don't have a pathway to the realization of our spiritual nature. Take some time now to close your eyes and just sit in silence for a few moments. [Silence.]

D: When you feel centered and fully present, please open your eyes and stand up.

What It's All About

[After some more minutes of silence R & R begin to hum a well known tune. They hum softly at first, and then louder and louder, inviting the group to join them.]

All: You put your right hand in, you put your right hand out, you put your right hand in and you shake it all about. You do the Hokey Pokey and you turn yourself around, that's what it's all about.

You put your left hand in, you put your left hand out, you put your left hand in and you shake it all about. You do the Hokey Pokey and you turn yourself around. That's what it's all about.

You put your right foot in, you put your right foot out, you put your right foot in and you shake it all about. You do the Hokey Pokey and you turn yourself around, that's what it's all about.

You put your left foot in, you put your left foot out, you put your left foot in and you shake it all about. You do the Hokey Pokey and you turn yourself around. That's what it's all about.

You put your whole self in, you put your whole self out, you put your whole self in and you shake it all about. You do the Hokey Pokey and you turn yourself around. That's what it's all about.

[Laughter and clapping.]

D: We trust that answers all of your questions.

"And Then a Miracle Happens"

D: I have a sweatshirt that Robert McDonald gave me showing a couple of men in white coats - scientist types. They're standing in front of a blackboard. And on the blackboard one of them has written a bunch of equations. At a certain point in the midst of all of this very scientific looking scribbling, he stops and writes, "And then a miracle happens." And then he madly goes on again with his equations. His colleague is pointing at the comment about the miracle and asking, "Could you be a bit more specific about that part there?"

In a way, I think that's a very basic metaphor for this program. I've written over a dozen books. Some of these books actually contain little equations that look a lot like the stuff this scientist was writing. Yet at some point it began to become very obvious to me that when something actually changes or heals it's not because of the equation or the specific sequence of steps in the technique; it's more like 'a miracle happens'.

"I THINK YOU SHOULD BE MORE EXPLICIT HERE IN STEP TWO."

Printed & Distributed by Cotton Expressions

© 1985. SIDNEY HARRIS

From my perspective, it was always a bit like: "You say some words, then you touch the person, you ask a few questions, have the person change his or her posture, then 'a miracle happens', then you say a few more words, have the person shift his or her posture again, and finish the steps of the technique." But the miracle that happens is not ultimately created or 'caused' by the technique. The technique is the ritual that goes on around the miracle.

Now this doesn't mean that the technical part, or the 'ritual', is not necessary or valuable. The technical part is like a tool, but the tool itself is not the experience.

In terms of my own work, Robert McDonald was the person who kept asking, "Can you be a little more explicit about the part where the miracle happens?" Robert was so persistent that I finally became intrigued by the question and we started looking for the answer together. We decided to be a little more explicit about 'the part where the miracle happens'. This seminar is a result of the attempt to answer that question.

Incidentally, seeking to answer this question doesn't take the miracle away. The miracle still happens somewhere and the understanding of it doesn't make it any less of a miracle.

And, as we were saying earlier, we believe that when you are exploring spiritual experience it is important to 'come home to' your body and be in your body. Spiritual experience is not in the equation, or on the chalk board, or in the head. The experience of spirit or of being in contact with spirituality is not something that happens only through the mind but also through the emotions and through the body.

M: I think making miracles also has something to do with being willing to let go of certain strongly held beliefs about how the world works. Maybe that's what "love" is about. We hope that what emerges in our *Tools of the Spirit* seminars is a context in which it's acceptable to communicate lovingly, talk about love, be involved in love and experience love.

The Two Lines Into Heaven

M: There is an illuminating story about a man who died and went to Heaven. He had lived a long life, and after he died he found himself walking toward these big pearly gates in front of heaven. At the gates he saw a number of people who are representative of the spirit - Buddha, Christ, His mother Mary, Saint Peter, Mohammed, Krishna, Moses and others who were standing at the gates letting people come in. As the man walked up to the gates he noticed that there were two lines to get into Heaven. He noticed that one line had about three or four people in it and the other line seemed to go on for miles. The man was confused by this. He wondered, "Why are there these two lines?" So he walked up to St. Peter and asked, "Can you help me out? I notice that there's this short line and this really long line and I'm not sure which line to get in. Why are some standing in the short line and others in the long line?" And St. Peter responded, "Well this line of three or four people would like to experience Heaven, and they are waiting to get in." And the man asked, "What about the long line of people?" And St. Peter said, "Oh, those people are interested in studying Heaven. They want to learn *about* it. They want to take notes." [Laughter]

Emphasis on Experience

M: It was important for me, in creating this program with Robert, to let go of having to know and to write everything down. What we have attempted to do with *Tools of the Spirit* is to create a context in which the emphasis is on experience as opposed to information.

D: The most important part of Tools of the Spirit is not the information that you will get on paper, it's the experience of when the "miracle" happens. And the best way to experience that is to involve yourself.

M: In our *Tools of the Spirit* seminars we ask people to speak from first person singular if they have something to say. We coach them to say, "I feel this", "I want this", "I notice this" "I experience that." As we have said, Robert and I are interested in assisting in the creation of a context in which as much and as great a change as possible can take place. That happens more readily in a context in which people own their own experience. And this is more likely to occur when people use 'I messages' such as, "This is what I feel, this is what I want, this is my experience."

D: We want to avoid the temptation to become stuck in philosophies or ideologies. These tend to lead to conflict and struggle. In contrast, we have found that when people actually feel and share experiences of spiritual connection and wholeness, they are not inclined to fight or argue. Spiritual experience is about unity and wholeness rather than right, wrong, good or bad.

For a long time I was one of the people standing in the mile long line, wanting to know about something before I experienced it. I didn't want to look like a fool or to be taken advantage of. I wanted to learn *about* "life" and "spirit". I wanted to have a map and an understanding of them.

Eventually, however, I was confronted by experiences that went beyond what I could describe or comprehend. Some of the ones that stand out to me in this moment are looking into the eyes of my father at the moment of his death and looking into the eyes of my son and daughter in the moments after they were born. These were experiences that couldn't be broken down or analyzed. They had to do with things that went beyond what I was sensing concretely. They involved the experience of something which was greater than myself and my interaction with these individuals.

I've had other experiences like that in my life. For example, at times when somebody is healing, I often have the experience that I am participating in something beyond myself. I may have an important role, but the source of the healing is something beyond what we typically call our "self".

Small "s" and Large "S" Self

D: This type of experience relates to what Robert and I call our small "s" and large "S" selves. The little "s" self is the part of ourselves that we tend to consciously show to others, and is the way we usually define ourselves. But there are moments, and I wonder whether you've had these moments, where we actually feel more present, or present in a different way. For instance, even though I'm my small "s" self in this moment, in this room, I can experience the presence of a me that's not only in this moment. It is a me that's always been and always will be. It is the presence of a me that's part of something bigger. It is this type of experience that is at the core of *Tools of the Spirit*. These experiences are often accompanied by a deep sense of joy, peace, belonging and connectedness.

M: I'm wondering how many of you have had an experience that you might describe as being "overtaken" or "overwhelmed" with Spirit. Take a moment and recall or reexperience one of these times. They are like a time of spiritual birth - of awakening to the unity and wonder of all things.

If you are like me, however, this experience of God or Spirit comes and goes. I'm not always able to stay connected with my larger "S" self. For example, I can be in the middle of doing the Hokey Pokey and suddenly think that I am doing something "wrong." Have you ever experienced something like that? I'll start to feel bad and make little corrections until I realize, "What am I doing here making this wrong? Everything's okay."

A Dream of the Large "S" Self

M: This reminds me of a dream I had many years ago in which I was running away from my brother. When I was a child my brother would hurt me quite a bit, physically and emotionally. My childhood was a typical story of an alcoholic family. My older brother could be very abusive. And in my dream, I was running and he was behind me, and I could feel this panic inside of me. I don't know if you've ever had those types of feelings in your life, but I was feeling panic. My brother was going to get me and hurt me. I was running and I was crying, "Help, help!"

Then an interesting thing happened in this dream. The faster I ran, the more I began to move my arms. My arms spread wider and wider, and pretty soon they became large brown bird wings. Then I flew. I left the Earth and flew into the air. My cries of "help, help" changed into "cheep, cheep," like a bird sound. As I went into the air, I *became* a giant bird. When I looked back to where I had been running, I saw the shape of the Earth. The Earth was small by this time and I could see my brother running after Robert. I flew higher and higher until I was able to have a vast perception of the world. And all at once it occurred to me that I had always been flying. I had always been this bird. I had never not been this bird. I had come from forever and was going to forever, but, from time to time, I would dream or hallucinate that I was something else. I would incarnate as Robert or somebody on the Earth. And the rules were that, whenever I incarnated, I would forget that I was really a bird. I would forget that I had always been the bird, and that I was always utterly safe.

What I learned from that dream is that there is no time in which I am not profoundly safe. Flying high, as my true self, I become aware of my vast spiritual nature, and that I am this big "S" Self.

Then, when I come into this body, it is easier for my small "s" self to emerge and for me to start to think that I have a "beginning" and an "end". I start thinking in finite and dualistic terms like "front and back", and "left and right", and "up and down", and " dark and light". And I forget that there is something much larger from which I actually derive.

This is another example of the kind of large "S" Self experience that we're talking about.

Uniting the Large "S" and Small "s" Selves

D: I think many of us have had this type of experience at some point in our lives. There are moments when we feel our spiritual heritage or the spiritual roots of our lives. And there are many other moments when we forget our spiritual nature. It is like Robert said, the rule was that when he came back into his body, he would forget that he was really a bird.

Part of the mission of *Tools of the Spirit* is to help us remember our larger "S" self. Then, rather than thinking, "Oh, I have to go out of my body to have a spiritual experience," the experience is one that you have in the body and it's one that you have more often.

We often put ourselves into the framework where we think, "Well, there's my day-to-day life and then there's this sort of spiritual thing that I have sometimes." Maybe for some of you this spiritual awareness occurs at church, or during special moments. But those experiences seem separate from your everyday reality. For many, the spirit and the flesh are different things, and are at odds with one another.

One of our beliefs is that it's possible to both stay in our bodies *and* live more from this bigger Self. We believe that there is a vast potential within us that is largely untapped - on many different levels. The idea of *Tools of the Spirit* is to develop ways to have a sense of "meaning", "love", and "grace" in our lives. Our goal is to provide tools that allow us to remember and to keep in contact with our larger "S" self.

Fear, Love and Forgiveness

M: We also need tools to help us discover and transform what is in the way of being fully in our larger "S" selves. I often ask myself, "What stops me from having or experiencing more love, grace, mercy, compassion, understanding, kindness? What stops me? What's in the way?" Most of the time I discover that "fear" is the center of whatever is in my way.

For a long time I felt that my work was to eradicate fear. I thought, "If dynamite doesn't work, try some NLP and get rid of that fear." Then one day I spoke to therapist Loic Jassy about my fear. He said something that really changed my life. He asked, "Have you ever thought about loving your fear?" It was really strange because I didn't have any place to put that idea. I thought, "Loving my fear? Let's see, where does that fit? No, that doesn't fit somehow." One of my greatest learnings has been to find the ability and the grace to love my fear.

One of the goals of *Tools of the Spirit* is to create a context in which it becomes possible to ask ourselves quite sincerely, "What did you think it was that needed to be loved anyway? What did you think it was that needed to be loved in your life? Did you think it was walks in the park on Sunday, ice cream, good times and hugs? Is that what needs to be loved? Is that what has been longing, searching, thirsting, hungering for your embrace?" In my life, what needs love is that which I fear, and my fear itself.

Jesus said, "Love your enemies." From my perspective, the idea of loving one's enemies is the most radical idea there is; and the most profound challenge there is. If I love my enemies then where are they? Who are they?

A lot of people think they have internal enemies. Pop psychology even talks about 'self-sabotage'. But if I have no inner enemy, if I love my inner enemies, then what happens to all of that?

Robert Dilts and I come from different personal and professional backgrounds, but we found that we share a common understanding. We both believe very deeply that "behind every behavior is a positive intention." Behind every behavior, thought, fantasy, action, there's a positive, universally acceptable and applaudable purpose which longs to bring us to a place of universal innocence.

I must say right away that, as we talk about this, it makes no rational sense. I'm aware that my rational mind says, "No, that can't be." But there's a nonrational part of me which is all about forgiveness. In order to go from fear to love, the bridge is forgiveness. It makes no rational sense to forgive anybody for anything. What makes rational sense is to wait until they deserve to be forgiven. But then we could wait for a long time. Maybe forever.

I think the experience of forgiveness is an example of when "a miracle happens."

Chapter 2

Co-Alignment

Overview of Chapter 2

- **Levels of Experience**
- **An Analogy to the Roots and Branches of a Tree**
- **"Neuro-Logical" Levels**
- **Level Co-Alignment**
- **Summary of Logical Level Co-Alignment Process**

Levels of Experience

D: To begin to build the bridge between the little "s" self and the large "S" self, and between fear and love, we need to "be a little more explicit" about how that miracle happens. One way to help build this bridge is to recognize that we have different levels of experience.

People often talk about responding to things on different 'levels'. For instance, someone might say that an experience was negative on one level but positive on another level. In our brain structure, language, and perceptual systems there are natural hierarchies or levels of experience. The effect of each level is to organize and control the information on the level below it. Changing something on an upper level would necessarily change things on the lower levels; changing something on a lower level could but would not necessarily effect the upper levels. Anthropologist Gregory Bateson identified four basic levels of learning and change - each level more abstract than the level below it but each having a greater degree of impact on the individual. These levels roughly correspond to:

'Spiritual'	Who Else? What Else?
	Vision & Purpose
A. *Who I Am* –	Who?
Identity:	Role & Mission
B. *My Belief System* –	Why?
Values, Meta Programs:	Motivation & Permission
C. *My Capabilities* –	How?
States, Strategies:	Perception & Direction
D. *What I Do* –	What?
Specific Behaviors:	Actions & Reactions
E. *My Environment* –	Where? When?
External Context:	Constraints & Opportunities

The *environment* level involves the specific external conditions in which our behavior takes place - the *where* and *when* of our experience. That is, I can walk around in a particular room and I can look out and see the objects, hear the sounds, smell the odors and feel the temperature of the air, and that's a certain level of my experience. My ability to sense the external environment is one level of experience and involves a particular part of my nervous system.

My ability to sense and coordinate my own body's *behavior* as I move through that external environment involves another level of experience and mobilizes a part of my nervous system that is deeper than my sense organs. It has to do with *what* I am doing.

Exploring more deeply, I can find that there are other levels of my experience that go beyond my perceptions and my behavior in a particular environment. My behaviors themselves are coming from "mental maps" and other internal processes that happen in my mind. This is a level of experience that goes beyond the immediate environment. I can make pictures of things that do not relate to the particular room I am in. I can remember conversations that I had with Robert five years ago. This level of experience has to do with my mental and intellectual capabilities. Behaviors without any inner map, plan or strategy to guide them are like knee jerk reactions, habits or rituals. At the level of *capability* we are able to select, alter and adapt a class of behaviors to a wider set of external situations. It involves *how* I am perceiving and directing my actions.

At the level of *beliefs and values* we encourage, inhibit or generalize a particular strategy, plan or way of thinking. Our beliefs and values transcend any particular thoughts. They have to do with *why* we think what we think and do what we do.

Identity, of course, consolidates whole systems of beliefs and values into a sense of self. It has to do with our experience of *who* we are. I remember looking at my children when they were first born and recognizing that they were definitely not simply 'blank slates'. They were born with their own personalities. Even before they had sensed much of their environment, coordinated their behavior, formed mental maps or established particular beliefs and values, they had an identity; their own special way of being in the world.

Finally, there is the level involving what we're calling *"spiritual"* experience. This relates to the larger "S" self experience: the sense of something that goes beyond our own image of ourselves, our values, beliefs, thoughts, actions or perceptions. It relates to *who and what else* is in the larger system.

In summary:

* *Environmental factors* determine the external opportunities or constraints a person has to react to. Answer to the questions **where?** and **when?**

* *Behavior* is made up of the specific actions or reactions taken within the environment. Answer to the question **what?**

* *Capabilities* guide and give direction to behavioral actions through a mental map, plan or strategy. Answer to the question **how?**

* *Beliefs* and *values* provide the reinforcement (motivation and permission) that supports or denies capabilities. Answer to the question **why?**

* *Identity* factors determine overall purpose (mission) and shape beliefs and values through our sense of self. Answer to the question **who?**

* *Spiritual* experiences relate to our perception of being part of a larger system that reaches beyond ourselves as individuals to our family, community and global systems. Answer to the question **who/what else?**

While each level is successively more removed from the content of our behavior and sensory experience, it actually has more and more widespread effect on our behavior and experience.

An Analogy to the Roots and Branches of a Tree

As an analogy, our identity is like the trunk of a tree - it is the core of our being. The trunk of a tree unfolds organically from a seed by growing a support network of unseen roots that reach deeply into the ground to provide strength and nourishment. It has another network of "roots" that reach into the light and air to provide nourishment of a different kind. The roots and branches of a tree both shape and are shaped by the ecology in which they exist. Similarly our identities are supported by internal, invisible "roots" in the form of neural networks which process our perception of our personal values, beliefs and capabilities as well as physical being and environment.

Externally, identity is expressed through our participation in the larger systems in which we participate: our family, professional relationships, community and the global system of which we are a member. Phenomena such as "healing," "joy," "compassion," "commitment" and "love" are "fruits" of the spirit as manifested through our identity and are expressed and strengthened through development, enrichment and growth of these two systems of "roots" - the unseen system of our neurology which grows in the soil of our bodies, and the leaves and branches of the larger family, community and global networks of which we are a part.

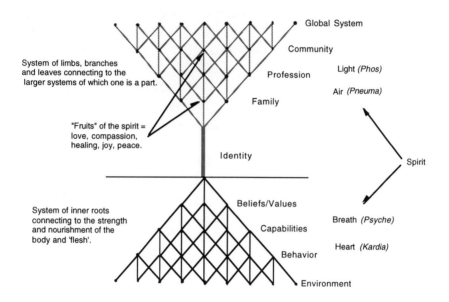

Levels of Experience

"Neuro-Logical" Levels

According to NLP, these various levels of our subjective experience are embodied in the form of neurological circuits. Each level mobilizes successively deeper and broader commitment of neurological 'circuitry'.

Environment: *Peripheral nervous system* - Sensations and reflex reactions.

Behaviors: *Motor system (pyramidal & cerebellum)* - Conscious actions

Capabilities: *Cortical systems* - Semi conscious actions (eye movements, posture, etc.)

Beliefs: *Autonomic nervous system* (e.g. heart rate, pupil dilation, etc.) - Unconscious responses.

Identity: *Immune system and endocrine system* - Deep life
 sustaining functions.

Spiritual: *Holographic* - Nervous system as a whole interacting with other nervous systems.

These various circuits may be activated and mobilized
through language patterns, cognitive strategies and behavioral cues. One way to think about getting stuck in the so-
called small "s" self is that we have become locked into only
one of these "neuro-logical" levels. For example, I had a day
last week that my wife was calling the 'day from Hell'. We
both got so caught up in the levels of behaviors and capabilities that we were trapped in the little "s" self all day. We lost
contact with the higher levels of our experience because we
were so focused on *doing* things. We lost our awareness of
and alignment with core beliefs and values. At such times, I
find myself doing things that don't fit with my own beliefs;
partially because I'm not in contact with those beliefs. I also
find myself doing things that seem to be in conflict with what
I perceive as my identity and mission. The question in those
times is, "How can we get access to the other levels of our
experience?"

Our first "tool" of the spirit, is a way of regaining and
maintaining alignment in those times when we discover that
we're trapped in the small "s" self. It is known as the Level
Alignment process.

Level Co-Alignment

D: The first form of "Level Alignment" we would like to demonstrate is one that actually helps to prevent becoming lost in the small "s" self in the first place. One of the things Robert and I like to do at the beginning of Tools of the Spirit is a procedure called *"co-alignment"*. In this process we reveal to each other and the group what is going on for us at each level of experience. We start at the level of environment and go all the way up to the level of spirit and vision.

We start in the environment because it is the most concrete level - the most immediately accessible. For instance, I'll look out at the room and I will share with Robert and the group what I'm noticing. I'll say, "When I look out at the environment, I notice the color of the walls. And I can see some pictures on the walls. I also notice flip charts in the front of the room with words on them. I notice that the sun is coming in through the windows. It's been cloudy up until now. I see little stripes of sun on the carpet. I am also aware of the people in the group. I mostly notice their eyes. Finally, I sense the temperature of the room. I can feel the air conditioner on my body and I can hear it. This is what's in my perception."

M: When Robert shares his perceptions with me I get a chance to have some sense of where he is and who he is. This also starts to enrich my perception. Before he said, "I mostly noticed eyes," I was seeing past people's eyes, and mostly focusing on the back of the room. I was aware of people's bodies, but not necessarily their eyes. When Robert mentioned "eyes" I realized, "Oh yes, there's all these eyes." So I've become more aware of what Robert is aware of.

Now it's my turn to share my perceptions of the environment with Robert.

I'm seeing the eyes, walls and sunlight now, but I'm also feeling the temperature of my hands. And I feel something drawing my attention over to one end of the room. I notice more empty space there. My attention is drawn there. So I have that pulling at me. When I heard Robert mention the sound of the air conditioning, I thought, "Yeah, I notice that." I notice the carpet, the walls and the people. I physically sense that there's space behind me, and I feel the floor under my feet.

D: This type of sharing serves several purposes for us. One is that it helps us to become more present; not only mentally but in the physical environment. Number two, as Robert describes his perceptions, it helps me and the group to understand and share where he's at, and what he is noticing. Number three, it expands my own perception. For instance, when Robert mentioned sensing the space behind him, I suddenly became aware of it. It had not been the slightest bit in my awareness before he said that.

Try this out for yourself. Take a moment and notice what stands out for you in your perception of the physical environment around you.

M: Keep in mind that this is simply your sensory perception of your environment. There isn't any judgment about what you are perceiving. Robert and I didn't say that we saw "beautiful" walls or "ugly" walls. At the environmental level there's no judgment. Judgments have to do with beliefs and values. Just notice what you perceive through your senses.

D: Once Robert and I have finished sharing our perceptions of the environment, we physically take a step back and share with each other how we want to act behaviorally in this environment. We answer the question, "How do I want to act in this time and place?" For example, I might say, "One of the things that's important for me to do in Tools of the Spirit is to keep my head, my heart and my body connected. This shows up behaviorally in the way that I use my hands. When all of these are connected my gestures are much more symmetrical. They are smooth rather than harsh gestures. And I tend to touch my body more.

I was noticing different group members giving each other hugs, and I feel like I'd like to have more physical contact with people in the group. It really helps me in this kind of seminar to touch people, shake hands, embrace them. I'd like to do more of that. And also when I think about you, Robert, there are ways that I want to act with you. When we are really tuned into each other it's like we're one person speaking and acting instead of two different people. That's how I'd like to be.

M: Yes, I understand that. What I want to be doing behavior-wise is moving with a greater fluidity. I feel a little tension, so I'd like to move with a little greater flexibility and move more from my center. I want to loosen up my belly. I want to have a softer belly and have softer knees so that I can be more present. I want to touch people more and be more involved - more kinesthetic, more touching, holding. I want to be open to that. I see myself actually going around and touching people physically and making contact. And there's a certain behavior I want with respect to my voice. I want my voice to come from a centered place; so that it's more aligned inside and more resonant.

D: As I'm listening to Robert and he's listening to me, we mirror or take on parts of each other's behavior. This helps us to get a better sense of how the other one wants to be. It also helps us to be a coach or a 'guardian angel' for one another.

Take a moment now and consider your own behavior. Get a sense of how you would be acting if you were aligned with your larger "S" self.

When we have finished sharing our behavioral outcomes, Robert and I take another step back to the level of "capability." At this level, we consider what skills and capabilities we need in order to be able to manifest the behaviors we have defined within the environment. We answer the question, "What kind of mental processes and cognitive skills do I have or need to have in order to mobilize and manifest my desired behavior in this time and place?"

As I consider that question, for example, I am aware that one of the capabilities I have and need more of is to sense my own inner state of congruence. I need to be able to sense whether I'm coming from a place that I would call "truth" or "centeredness". I need to be able to tell whether I'm completely present in a particular moment. There's a skill that's involved that has to do with an awareness of myself; of my body, my mind, and of hearing my own voice. Sometimes it's easy for me to stop hearing myself but keep talking. And it's important for me to be able to hear what I'm saying,

M: It sounds like a type of skillful presence.

D: Yes. And there are also skills that relate to the interaction between myself and others. There are skills that have to do with being able to invite people to ask questions; to help people feel safe enough to be able ask questions; to feel stimulated enough to want to know more; and to be able to express themselves and bring more of themselves here and now. These skills have to do with my rapport with the group. And then with you, Robert, there's the skill of being able to get into the special kind of rapport that occurs between our two larger "S" selves.

M: Yes, I know what you mean. It is a special type of flow. I want that with you too. For me, I need the skill of letting go of something. I also want to have my inner voice and pictures to be more gentle with me. When I can do that, my behavior starts to change. I begin to breathe a little deeper. The state that I want is that of bringing down a defense; becoming defenseless, like "It's just me." Nothing special, just me, whatever's here. I feel like I don't have to make a presentation, but rather just be here. And that comes out of the ability to let things melt around me. This makes it more okay for me to connect up with you and the group. I want that.

D: Again, having shared with each other which skills we need in order to act the way we want, we can be better guardian angels to one another.

　　The next phase of the 'co-alignment' process is to step back to the level of beliefs and values. At this level we consider the reasons why we want to mobilize these skills we have just identified and act in the way that we have defined. We share with each other and the group our beliefs and values related to *Tools of the Spirit*. We answer the question, "What are the beliefs and values that are important for me to manifest through my skills and actions in this time and place?"

　　One important belief for me, for instance, is that when I am able to be congruent and be in my large "S" self, it naturally makes a space for others to do the same. A second belief is that what Robert and I do in Tools of the Spirit has a broader influence than the specific time and place in which we are acting. It's the belief that the healing we do through Tools of the Spirit can also create healing in other places. So that what we accomplish in *Tools of the Spirit* isn't limited to a particular context.

　　Another belief that's important for me is that wherever I am when I do *Tools of the Spirit* is a sacred place and is the most important place for me to be on this planet at this moment. When I have the beliefs that where I am is the most important place for me to be at this moment, and that what I am doing has a broader influence, then I can be completely present in my large "S" self.

M: One of the beliefs that I want to have and experience during *Tools of the Spirit* is that by being emotionally transparent, others will tend to become transparent themselves. I want to have that belief present in me. And I want to have the belief that being defenseless is not dangerous to my core; that my core is never in danger. There may be surface level pains, struggles and hurts, but internally my core is never damaged because it's connected with all beings. It is all right for me to be fully present when I have these beliefs. And it's all right for me to stumble and ...

D: And make a mistake on the Hokey Pokey? [Laughter]

M: Make a lot of mistakes.

D: And it doesn't affect your core.

M: And it doesn't affect my core. Imperfection is part of the deal. Yeah, I want to believe that.

D: Once we have shared our beliefs with one another, and the group, we take another step back to the level of identity. The question we answer at this level is, "If I have these perceptions of the environment, and act in the ways I have defined, and use the skills I have identified in order to manifest the beliefs and values that I have stated, then who am I?" We typically find that this question is best answered through the use of a symbol or metaphor.

The symbol or metaphor that emerges for me in this moment is of a magic wand with multi-colored threads of light going out.

M: For me, I had an image of a banana being peeled, which then became an onion being peeled, and I ended up with the symbol of an artichoke. You peel away the leaves to get to the heart of the artichoke. The sense is of something that is opening to a place that is soft and defenseless.

D: So you are like an artichoke that opens to reveal its heart.

M: Yes.

D: After we have shared our metaphors for our identities, we step back to the spiritual level; a place that is beyond ourselves. We step back beyond our perceptions of our environment, and beyond our behaviors, capabilities, beliefs, values and our sense of self, to our experience of the larger system of which we are a part. The question here is, "What is my vision of the larger system of which I am a part and which gives me purpose and meaning?"

What comes to me is a vision that has something to do with healing but also melting. Not healing in terms of fixing, but there's a kind of a warmth that goes out. I know that light is commonly used as a representation of spiritual processes. But my feeling is of a warmth that goes along with the light. This warmth or heat is able to transform things. For instance, when you cook something, it often becomes softer. Some things change into another form when they are warmed or heated. Something can be a problem in one form and then you heat it and it becomes edible or usable. So my vision is of a warmth which spreads out into the universe.

M: A spreading warmth. I like that.

When I go to this spiritual place, and consider my larger mission, I have a sense of something much broader than myself. It is broader than I am and it connects more fully than I do. It's like arms opening - bird wings that open - creating more room and possibilities. The purpose of these wings and this space is to heal and be healed. It comes again and again. Healing and being healed. The purpose of the wings is to touch and to reach out and embrace the world. That's the vision.

D: Wings that embrace the world in order to heal and be healed. That is a powerful image.

Now that we've shared our experience at all of these different levels, our next step is to combine our two visions together. We attempt to synthesize my warmth and Robert's embrace. For example, as I think about doing that, I get a sense of something like a warm embrace.

M: I also have the sense of warm air rising up allowing the wings to float into the air and fly. It's as if the heat helps create buoyancy for the wings.

D: I feel the way I feel when I embrace my children. There's warmth, and there's also something that goes far beyond the physical warmth. There is a certain type of deep contact that is transmitted through the embrace.

M: The contact is in the embrace and the warmth combined.

D: Once we have combined our visions, we return to the identity space, bringing our sense of our shared vision.

M: And we ask the question, "Who are we together?"

D: We bring the sense of the integration of the warmth and the embrace into our respective identities: the wand with colored threads of light and an artichoke. Then we ask, "Given our combined vision, who are we together that is more than merely a wand and an artichoke?"

M: I experience the artichoke changing into a lotus that is opening and very colorful.

D: I imagine the colors emanating out, sort of like a lotus of light.

M: A lotus of light that is opening and spreading warmth.

D: Next, we take the sense of our joint vision and identity and we return to the location for beliefs and values. Here, we ask, "What are the beliefs that we share and bring to life together here in this place with this group? What are the beliefs that are important in relation to this 'lotus of light'? And it seems to me there are shared beliefs and values related to healing and making this a sacred space.

M: And the belief that it really can be done. This can be done. This is just human. I have a very strong feeling of bringing this lotus of light here and believing that we can heal. We can be healed. We can connect. It is possible. It's not outside the realm of possibility, and we can do it here.

D: It's like the miracle can happen here.

M: Yes. The miracle *can* happen here.

D: After we have explored our shared beliefs and values, we step forward to the capabilities location and ask, "What are the capabilities that we have together that we do not have as individuals? What is it that we are capable of together that we're not capable of by ourselves?"

M: It's the interweaving of being skillfully present and letting go.

D: One of the things we do together is to create a context of sufficient safety and intimacy so that others can also be present and let go. We can co-create a context of possibility where people can be their large "S" self – a context where they can do things that they might not normally allow themselves to do, or give themselves the permission to do. I think that's a capability that we have together.

M: It's like this colorful lotus is nurturing and inviting on one hand, but is also directed and impactful. So it's not just one or the other. We can be transformative in a gentle way, but transformative nonetheless.

D: Yes. Our next step is to return to the 'behavior' location and ask, "How does this alignment of vision, identity, beliefs, values and capabilities, manifest through our behavior together? How does this very abstract idea of a 'lotus of light' come out in how we talk, move, act, look at people, touch people, etc.?"

M: I feel very strongly now that it is much more possible to touch and to connect with people. Touching and being with people and opening my breathing is much more possible.

D: I feel my voice changing. I have a sense of a voice that's coming from both of us, not just me, even though it's coming out of my mouth. It's like clearing a space for something to happen.

M: It creates an opening. It becomes possible to open. To me, it's as if our behaviors come out of two "I's" that have become "we". And in the "we", something else happens.

D: Our final step is to take all of these aligned and integrated levels of experience back into the environment, and notice how our perception of it has changed.

M: If you have been following along with us, we invite you to do the same thing.

D: For me, I notice that when I look around, the environment appears more 3-dimensional. More things seem within my reach. Instead of just seeing eyes, I see bodies. I see feet. I see people breathing. My peripheral vision has widened significantly.

M: It's not only more 3-dimensional for me but also more internal. I see much more inside, and it's a lot brighter within me now. Instead of projecting my own fear, I'm seeing what's there. There's more love.

D: Instead of just 'seeing' a bunch of eyes, I sense 'eye' ("I") contact.

M: Good.

D: One purpose of this demonstration has been to give you a sense of each of the different levels. We wanted to show how they are different and how they can become aligned. It is a way to create access to your larger "S" self.

M: Another reason that we go through the co-alignment process is to be more fully present with you, and help all of you to become more fully present.

D: Initially, Robert and I would do this process with ourselves in our hotel room in order to prepare ourselves spiritually to do "Tools of the Spirit". Then at one point we wondered, "Why are we doing this by ourselves? The group should be involved in this as well, because that's going to tell them more about what 'Tools of the Spirit' is and what's going to happen than what's in their booklets."

By observing us align ourselves, you not only get a better sense of what we mean by each of these levels, you get an opportunity to 'vicariously' become more aligned yourself.

Summary of Logical Level Co-Alignment Process

1. Physically lay out two spaces for each of the six logical levels.

Environment	Behaviors	Capabilities	Beliefs/Values	Identity	Spiritual
Environment	Behaviors	Capabilities	Beliefs/Values	Identity	Spiritual

2. Stand together in the "Environment" spaces and identify an environment (a place and time) that you share. Describe your perception of that environment to each other.

3. Stand in the "Behavior" space and answer the question: "What do I want to do when I am in that time and place?" Describe to each other some specific behaviors and actions that you want to manifest in your shared environment.

4. Stand in the "Capabilities" space and describe to each other the capabilities you have or need to have in order to manifest those actions in that environment.

5. Stand in the "Beliefs/Values" space and answer the question: "Why do I want to use those particular capabilities to accomplish those activities?" Disclose to each other the values and beliefs that are reflected in the capabilities and behaviors you want to manifest in your shared environment, and which motivate you to use those abilities.

6. Stand in the "Identity" space and answer the question: "Who am I that I have these motivations and capabilities to manifest those behaviors in that environment? What is a metaphor for my identity?" Using a metaphor verbalize your perception of yourself in relation to the

beliefs, values, capabilities and behaviors you have identified.

7. Stand in the "Spiritual" space and answer the question: "What is the larger vision and purpose I am pursuing or representing?" Describe to each other your visions of the larger system in which you are participating.

8. Explore the ways the two visions fit together or complement each other. Together, take that physiology and inner experience and step back into the identity space so you experience both at the same time. Answer the questions, "Who are we together?" "What is our joint identity?"

9. Take your shared experience of both your vision and your identity and bring them into your belief spaces. Answer the question, "What are our shared beliefs and values?"

10. Bring Your vision, identity, beliefs and values into the capabilities space. Answer the question, "What capabilities do we have as a team that are beyond our individual capabilities?"

11. Bring your vision, identity, beliefs, values and capabilities into the behavior space. Notice how even the most insignificant seeming behaviors are reflections and manifestations of all of the higher levels within you. Answer the question, "What will be our joint actions together?"

12. Bring all levels of yourself into the environment space and experience how it is transformed and enriched.

Chapter 3

Sacred Journey

Overview of Chapter 3

- The Sacred Journey Process
- An Image of the Large 'S' Self
- Introductions Using Drawings of the Large "S" Self
- Map and Territory

The Sacred Journey Process

M: The process of level alignment is like preparing the ground before planting the seed.

D: We'd like to give you an opportunity to align yourselves individually in the form of a meditation that we call the 'Sacred Journey'. In this process you take a journey through these different levels within yourself and align them.

M: Earlier I asked you to think about your own personal experience of "spirit". I asked you to identify times in your life when you felt the almost overwhelming presence of something much greater than yourself; perhaps something that has an unreasonable love for you. Maybe you've never experienced that. Or, perhaps, when you were a little boy or girl you had a time in your life when you were able to open up to something that you couldn't describe or articulate, something that was much larger than yourself.

D: Perhaps you've had the sense that you were unconditionally loved by something bigger than yourself.

M: Sometimes I ask myself the question, "How many times have I cut my hand and it's been healed? How many times have I had a mosquito bite and it's been healed? And how much of that healing did I create? How much of it did I make happen?" Did I say to my body, "Heal," and suddenly my hand was healed? There is something that heals us and has always healed us since we were little children. How could you have come this far in life and not been healed again and again? There is something which has always come to your aid. Always. And the evidence of this is that you are alive. You might want to keep this in the back of your mind as you go through this process.

D: To start, sit with your legs uncrossed and put your feet flat on the floor. You may want to take your shoes off. Make sure that your hands can easily touch your legs, belly, diaphragm, chest, throat and face. For this exercise you will need to make contact with all of these different areas of your body.

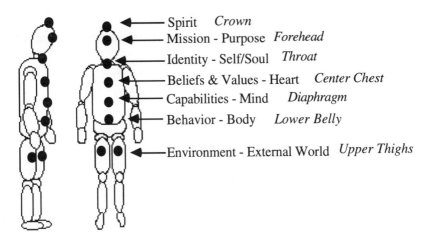

Spirit *Crown*
Mission - Purpose *Forehead*
Identity - Self/Soul *Throat*
Beliefs & Values - Heart *Center Chest*
Capabilities - Mind *Diaphragm*
Behavior - Body *Lower Belly*
Environment - External World *Upper Thighs*

Location of 'Touch Anchors' For Sacred Journey Process

1. In an emotional state of reverence and meditation, sit in a 'neutral' or 'resting' position with your feet on the floor and your hands folded comfortably in your lap.

2. Close your eyes and become aware of your *external environment*. Think of other environments (home, work, social, global) into which you would like to bring a 'spiritual healing' or more of a sense of 'spiritual presence' or connection. When you have this environment in mind, place your hands palm down on your *upper legs* or thighs. Allow your touch to communicate your intention to 'heal', 'sanctify' or 'cleanse' this environment. Then, return your hands to the 'neutral/resting' position in your lap.

3. Allow your attention to shift to your *physical body and behavior*. Sense any parts of your body, or any specific behaviors, into which you would like to bring a 'spiritual healing' or more of a sense of 'spiritual presence' or connection. As you internally feel this part of your body, or sense what it is like when you do the specific behavior, allow your hands to move up and touch your *lower belly*, just below your naval. Allow your touch to communicate your intention to 'heal', 'sanctify' or 'cleanse' this part of your body or behavior. Then, return your hands to the 'neutral/resting' position in your lap.

4. Now become aware of your *mind and thoughts*, noting any that are confused or limiting. Focus on any thoughts or parts of your mind into which you would like to bring a 'spiritual healing' or more of a sense of 'spiritual presence' or connection. As you focus on these thoughts or parts of your mind, allow your hands to move up and touch your *diaphragm*, just below your chest bone where your ribs join together. Allow your touch to communicate your intention to 'heal', 'sanctify' or 'cleanse' these thoughts or parts of your mind. Then, return your hands to the 'neutral/resting' position in your lap.

5. Turn your attention to your *beliefs and belief system*. Find any negative or painful beliefs or parts of your belief system into which you would like to bring a 'spiritual healing' or more of a sense of 'spiritual presence' or connection. As you focus on these beliefs, allow your hands to move up and touch your *heart* area, at the center of your chest. Allow your touch to communicate your intention to 'heal', 'sanctify' or 'cleanse' these beliefs or parts of your belief system. Then, return your hands to the 'neutral/resting' position in your lap.

Repeat and acknowledge your 'journey' up to this point by touching your legs, your lower belly, your diaphragm and your heart. Then, return your hands once again to the 'neutral/resting' position in your lap.

6. Shift your awareness to your *identity and sense of self*. Notice any parts of you that are angry, lost, left behind, abused or somehow separated from you. Concentrate on the part of yourself into which you would like to bring a 'spiritual healing' or more of a sense of 'spiritual presence' or connection. As you focus on this part of yourself, allow your hands to move up and gently touch the *base of your throat*. Allow your touch to communicate your intention to 'heal', 'sanctify' or 'cleanse' this part of yourself. Then, return your hands to the 'neutral/resting' position in your lap.

7. Now become aware of your *'mission' or higher 'purpose'*. Think about what interferes with or separates you from fully pursuing your mission or fulfilling your purpose in life. Concentrate on whatever is keeping you from your mission or purpose into which you would like to bring a 'spiritual healing' or more of a sense of 'spiritual presence' or connection. As you focus on these interferences, allow your hands to move up and touch the *center of your forehead*. Allow your touch to communicate your intention to 'heal', 'sanctify' or 'cleanse' these interferences. Then, return your hands to the 'neutral/resting' position in your lap.

Repeat and acknowledge your 'journey' up to this point by touching your legs, your lower belly, your diaphragm, your heart, the base of your throat and the center of your forehead.

8. Now, raise your hands above your head and open your arms, opening yourself to a *deep source of spiritual healing* (i.e., 'spirit', 'universal mind', 'Christ consciousness', 'God', etc.). Invite and receive into you the healing 'energy' from that source. Using your hands to 'gather' this energy, bring it into your body through the *crown of your head*.

9. Allow your hands to gently retrace the steps of your 'sacred journey', bringing this healing spiritual energy to each 'step' on your path. Move your hands down your body slowly, touching the center of your forehead, the base of your throat, your heart, diaphragm, lower belly and finally your legs. Feel this energy filling each location, flowing through your whole body and out into the environment through your feet. You may move your hands back to any position on which you would like to focus or concentrate.

10. When you are done, return your hands to the 'neutral/ resting' position in your lap and spend some time feeling and acknowledging your sense of alignment, wholeness and healing.

Notice that while in this state you can be fully in touch with your large "S" Self. As you feel a sense of spiritual connection and the presence of your larger self, allow an image or a symbol to emerge in your mind's eye that represents this feeling. If this feeling could become an image that you could see, what would it be? Say to yourself, "This feeling is like..." and notice what naturally emerges to complete the sentence.

When you have an image, get some colored pencils, pens or crayons and draw a picture of your image or symbol on the following page (or on another piece of paper).

An Image of the Large 'S' Self

Draw your picture of your large 'S' self in the space above.

Introductions Using Drawings of the Large "S" Self

D: In our *Tools of the Spirit* workshop, we ask people to sign their drawings when they are finished with them.

M: We then ask them to hold their drawings up so that the drawings can be seen by other people.

D: We point out that these images are as much of a representation of themselves as what they see in the mirror. What you see in the mirror is the reflection of the "surface structure" of your smaller "s" self. These pictures are reflections of the "deep structure" of your large "S" self.

M: These pictures are representative of something that's largely inarticulable. What they have drawn has meaning for themselves and what they see has meaning for other people. Keeping that in mind, we ask everyone to take a few moments to wander around silently looking at each other's drawings.

D: Next, we ask people to form groups of about 4 or 5 people each and introduce themselves to each other through their drawings.

M: For instance, if Robert and I were in a smaller group, and I were introducing myself to Robert, I'd say something like, "Hi, I'm Robert. I am this flowing energy that's coming out in blues and purples and there's some gold. When I am my large 'S' self, I am expansively energetic from every direction. My energy is just flowing out. I'm an energy being."

D: The other group members may then ask questions about the drawing. For example, I might say, "Robert, I notice that it looks like the energy flows differently in different parts of your being. Is that intentional?"

M: Yes. There's a lot more energy in my face than in my arms or legs. It is as if it collects in my heart and explodes out of my face. It flows out in many different directions.

Now inwardly there's a small "s" self inside of me saying, "Oh, but I didn't mean *that* when I drew it. My small "s" self wants to contradict what I've said.

D: The small "s" self can get stuck on the surface structure and want to try to explain it, rather than stay with the deeper structure.

M: The small "s" self wants to say, "Well, if I were Michelangelo it would really look right." But it looks exactly right. What you've drawn is it. Just go with it rather than try to deny it or try to explain it away. Say, "Yeah, here I am. Isn't that interesting. I've got all this energy emerging from me and there's more collected in my face."

D: Incidentally, notice that, when he introduced himself, Robert didn't say, "This is a picture I drew of me and it shows energy flowing in all directions." He said, "I am this energy flowing in all directions".

As another example, if I were to introduce myself through my drawing, I would say, "Hi, my name's Robert too. I am a magic wand of many different colors and energies. One of the things that's important about me is that I am being held by something. The hand holding me is an important part of being in my large 'S' self. It is significant that I am the wand, not the color that's coming out from me or the hand that is holding me.

M: You're a wand that is being held, and out of you comes this colorful energy.

D: Yes.

M: As with me, the members of our group could ask questions about Robert's drawing.

C: Is the color when the miracle happens?

D: The miracle actually happens somewhere in between the hand, the wand and the color.

C: It's all together.

D: Yes. The miracle is the fact that there's colors coming out of the wand to begin with.

Again, notice that I am not merely talking about my picture, I am talking about myself. And as Robert pointed out, we don't want to get caught up in the detail of the picture. What you're doing is talking about you. It's quite different than talking about the picture.

When people have finished their introductions, have them put their pictures up on the wall. This way, all of the large "S" drawings are surrounding the room. They serve as a reminder or "anchor" for all of the experiences of the large "S" selves.

Map and Territory

Sometimes we will have people look around the room at all of these remarkable pictures and humorously ask, "I wonder which one is the right map of the presence of spirit?" In our view, arguing about whose map of the large "S" self is the one "true" map is like fighting a religious war. Your sense of your large "S" Self is a personal experience.

The level of "spirit" goes beyond behaviors and beliefs. A religious institution is an attempt to embody a spiritual experience in the form of beliefs and behaviors. It is important to keep in mind, however, that these beliefs and behaviors are surface structures which attempt to embody a deeper, more experiential structure.

One of the important presuppositions of 'Tools of the Spirit' is the NLP principle that "the map is not the territory." No matter what map we draw or what descriptions we give, it's not going to be the territory. Our experience is going to be closer to that deeper structure.

Chapter 4

Presence of Eternity

Overview of Chapter 4

- **Presence of Eternity**

- **Time Lines and "Anchoring"**

- **"Whenever Two or More Are Gathered in My Name"**

- **The Presence of Eternity Process**

- **Summary of 'The Presence Of Eternity' - Integrating Time Frames**

The Presence of Eternity

D: Traditional "tools of the spirit" involve activities like prayer, meditation, ritual, singing, dancing and poetry. These are processes by which people are able to express spiritual aspects of themselves and become more aligned, connected with, or in touch with spiritual aspects of their experience.

When Robert and I were first creating the Tools of the Spirit program, we asked ourselves, "What could NLP add to the search for more spiritual wholeness in our lives?" And we wondered, "What are some of the tools that NLP offers that have not yet been considered as spiritual tools?" For instance, 'prayer' is a 'neurolinguistic' activity. 'Singing' is also neurolinguistic. Dancing is not so 'linguistic', but it certainly is 'neuro'.

But some of the other tools that we have in NLP are processes like 'anchoring' and 'submodalities'. Of course, the way that you would apply these processes to enhance a spiritual level experience is different than the way you'd use them to achieve a specific outcome on a behavioral level.

Time Lines and "Anchoring"

One common tool of NLP is the notion of a 'time line', and our perception of time. For example, think of the "now." How do you know that it is 'now'? How big is the now? When you think of 'now', is it large or is it small? When you think about time, which direction is the 'past' and which direction is the 'future'. For example, is the past behind you, to your left, or somewhere else?

Behaviors, for instance, are very much related to linear time. All concrete actions have a start, a middle and a finish. Walking, for example, involves moving your legs in a very specific order, which can be measured with respect to time. Particular behaviors take place sequentially with respect to time. In this type of time perception, the present is experienced as a point along a line that extends from the past to the future. Often, the past is behind you, the future is in front of you.

Beliefs and values, however, are not so much related to linear time. Values and beliefs do not manifest in a sequential progression of steps like a tennis serve or a football game. You believe in something or you do not. You value something or you do not. For instance, you believe you can walk, or you believe that you are a good tennis player. Beliefs may change, or there may be varying degrees of belief, or hierarchies of values, but this is not related to a specific linear progression. Beliefs and values are more detached from a particular segment of time. Likewise, spiritual experiences are very rarely encoded in terms of linear time. In fact, spiritual experiences are typically characterized by a very altered perception of time, such as having a sense of "timelessness"

One of the things that Robert McDonald and I explored in developing *Tools of the Spirit* was whether we could use time lines in order to help connect with spiritual level experiences in our everyday lives.

Our perception of 'time' often influences the way we give meaning to an experience You probably all have noticed that there have been moments when something seems so important at a particular moment; but when you consider it in a larger time frame, you think, "Why was I so caught up in that?"

To bring more of the spiritual into our lives, we need the awareness of multiple perspectives of time. I know in my own experience that healing cannot take place without the energy of the present. Healing doesn't happen in a timeless way. It happens in relation to time. You need the energy of the 'now' to produce change. But you also need the wisdom of 'forever', the wisdom of eternity, to ensure that change is ecological.

Eternity is very wise, but it's very diffuse. The present has a lot of energy, a lot of activity, but has a limited perspective. What gives something meaning is often the wisdom of forever.

M: This is similar to "being and "doing". On the one hand we have being, on the other hand doing. "Being" by itself doesn't produce an end result. And "doing" by itself produces end results, but has no inherent meaning. The combination of "being" and "doing", the combination of the "heart" and the "sword", produces something together that is not possible if they are separated.

D: We would like to lead you through a process, based on a format that I orginally developed with Todd Epstein, that we call the "presence of eternity" or "now and forever." This exercise uses two NLP tools: that of time perception, the time line, and the tool of 'anchoring'.

M: Keep in mind that all NLP tools, and NLP itself is useless without an outcome. NLP is absolutely pointless without wanting something. If I 'sort of' want something, then I can 'sort of' use NLP to 'sort of' get it. And if I'm 'sort of' involved in this exercise then I can 'sort of' get some results. But if you make a decision to give yourself completely to the exercise and to discovering what's there, you'll get a chance to experience the results of complete transformation or complete giving.

When I pray before coming to do this work, and while presenting the *Tools of the Spirit* course, I ask God, in Christ's name, to help me be generous. I pray to give away as much as I can, and to deal with my own fears and limitations through generosity - by giving away and noticing that what I give is returned to me, multiplied many times. In a moment you will have an opportunity to give yourself to something that is transformative.

D: We sometimes talk about a 'tool of the spirit' as being similar to a 'bridge'. A bridge is like a tool. When you walk across the bridge, you end up on the other side. If you become enamored with the bridge, then you will become caught up with the tool itself.

M: So notice that the 'tool' is not the experience.

"Whenever Two or More Are Gathered in My Name"

D: To do this exercise you need to have a partner. The Sacred Journey is an activity you can do by yourself. But some forms of spiritual awareness cannot be experienced in isolation. You experience them in relationship with others. For instance, Jesus said, "Whenever two or more are gathered in my name, there also am I." I have always thought that this indicated something very profound about the nature of spiritual experience. The implication of Jesus' comment is that spiritual awareness is something that is generated between people somehow. That is why Robert and I teach Tools of the Spirit together. It's not because we would forget what to do if we were by ourselves. We've done the program so many times that we know all of the pieces. Rather, it's because there's something that is created in our interaction that we cannot create by ourselves in the same way. So this involves having a partner.

M: Consider who you'd like to partner up with. As you read this, imagine a significant other in your life. It could be somebody you've known for a long time. It could be somebody new. Have you ever looked at someone and noticed just the outside of the person, and then made a deliberate decision to see inside of him or her? Have you ever noticed that within each person is a living flame? Have you ever deliberately looked past the surface level to discover what is fundamentally the same between you and other people?

D: This is like looking at the surface structure of somebody, and then looking at their deeper structure. During this exercise you will be standing up and facing a significant other, at about arm's length.

The Presence of Eternity Process

M: Begin by facing your partner (or imagine you are facing that person).

D: Place yourself at a close but comfortable distance from one another. Make sure that you are in good rapport and feel safe.

M: This is essentially a nonverbal exercise. So it is important to remain silent as you follow our instructions.

D: Once you are in rapport with your partner, mirroring each another, then close your eyes. As you do, begin to experience yourself fully in the present. Be totally in the 'here and now'. Feel your feet firmly on the ground, now.

M: Notice your breathing, now. What is it like to be in the 'now'? "Now" passes quite quickly, doesn't it?

D: Connect with the present. Come into the energy of the "now." Enter into the experience that nothing else is important except what's happening right now in the immediate moment.

M: Pay attention to the sounds and feelings of 'now'.

D: Be in your body, so that you feel fully present in this moment, not in your head, in the past or in the future.

There is no need to think about yesterday or tomorrow. Pay attention only to what's happening in this moment. When you have the sense of being 'here and now', fully in this moment, then you can allow your eyes to begin to open.

M: Keeping the sense of now.

D: Look into your partner's eyes.

M: Notice which eye seems to be the most appropriate to look into in order to stay in the now. Is it the left eye, or the right eye? If you find yourself moving away to the past or future, just bring your attention back to here and now.

D: Be in your body, fully present, perhaps noticing the slight moisture on your partner's eyes and how it reflects the light. And when you're able to look at your partner and stay right now in this moment, you can extend your right hand and gently hold the hand of the other person.

M: Just grasp or clasp right hands, without shaking them. Just clasp hands and continue to look in the eyes of your partner, staying completely in the present moment.

D: Really feel your partner's hand. Notice the temperature and the softness or firmness of the hand.

M: You can intensify the sense of now by opening your eyes just slightly, just the slightest amount.

D: Keep feeling the energy of the present, the energy of the now, and continue feeling your connection with the other person.

M: Right now with this person, notice the feeling of your hand and their hand as you look in their eyes. Be aware of your breathing.

D: When you've made that connection in the energy of the now, you can respectfully and gently release hands.

M: And close your eyes.

D: And then do the Hokey Pokey, turn yourself about.

M: Now face your partner again, and when you are ready, close your eyes. But this time begin to notice that this moment is a part of a larger frame of time.

D: Expand your sense of 'now' to include this morning all the way to the end of the day. This moment right now is one moment in a much larger frame of time that started this morning and will end tonight.

M: And of course this particular day is a smaller part of an even larger frame. Expand your sense of time to include the point when you first became aware that there was something called "Tools of the Spirit."

D: This present moment is actually a result of a process that started much earlier, when you made the decision to explore "Tools of the Spirit." It is part of a process that will continue on into the future, even after you finish this exercise and return to your everyday reality.

M: Expand your sense of time to include last week, the weeks before that, and several weeks from now.

D: Widen your awareness of time even further. There are experiences in your life that started several months ago and will continue for months into the future. This particular moment is just one in a much larger frame of time in your life.

M: The present moment is only a small part of a certain period in your life. Perhaps this larger period of time includes the previous 5 years and the next 5 years. Perhaps you are at a stage in your life that extends from 10 years ago to 10 years into the future.

D: Continue to widen your sense of time until you realize that, even though you're standing here now, there are many things that have happened in your life that brought you here, and many other things that have yet to occur in the years to come. Expand your awareness to include your childhood. In a way, this moment is part of something that started in your childhood, and will go on until you become much older than you are now.

M: Expand your sense of time to include your entire life, from birth to death. This moment is just one tiny particle in a much vaster ocean of time.

D: Perhaps you can even expand your awareness of time to extend beyond your own life. Include the lifetimes of your parents, and your parents' parents.

M: And their parents.

D: Also extend your sense of time into the future.

M: Include the lifetimes of the children that have yet to be born, and of their children, and their children's children, on into the future. Also be aware of all the time that passed before the human race emerged.

D: This one moment, right now, is part of something that started long before you were born.

M: It's always been coming.

D: And will go on years and perhaps even generations and ages after this. What you do here will have an influence a thousand, and even ten thousand years from now.

M: Perhaps you will even be able to expand your sense of time to include the beginning of time. Before there was time. Before there were planets, a solar system, or a universe.

D: Expand your sense of time to the infinite. Realize that this moment is just one grain of sand in infinity of other moments.

M: Expand your sense of time beyond any sense of time you've had before.

D: When you're able to have the sense that this moment is just one speck in a vast and wise eternity of time, gently open your eyes again and look at your partner.

M: Look at your partner from this perspective, this knowledge of that vast eternity of time.

D: Be open to the 'wisdom of forever'. Notice which eye you look into now. Which of your partner's eyes is most appropriate to look into in order to stay in the experience of eternity? Is it the same eye as before, or is it the other eye? Notice how deeply you are willing to look.

M: Perhaps it's far deeper than you ever imagined. Notice that all of this has always been coming, and will continue far beyond this moment.

D: When you're able to experience the sense of meeting together and connecting within the vastness of forever, please extend your left hand towards your partner.

M: Clasp your left hand with your partner's left hand. Hold hands while continuing to look into the eyes of the other person. It's as though two enormous galaxies come together for a moment in this vast eternity of space and time. Breathe into this eternity. Feel it in your body. Expand your awareness into your sense of forever.

D: When you've made this connection with your partner and the wisdom of forever, you can then gently release hands.

M: Allow your eyes to close, as your hands come back to your sides.

D: And then once again do the Hokey Pokey, turn yourself around.

M: Shift your state a little bit, and then face your partner.

D: By clasping hands during these experiences of "now" and "forever," you have established a pair of very important 'anchors'. Once anchors have been established, they can be 'integrated'. In silence, face each other again. And this time clasp both hands.

M: Looking into each other's eyes, take each other's hands.

D: Right hand to right hand, left hand to left hand.

M: Notice the joining of the experiences of both 'now' and 'forever'.

D: Allow a space to be created somewhere in between you. A space that is in between now and forever. When you feel this space, invite into it three wishes or intentions for spiritual healing.

M: These could be three prayers, wishes, or intentions. One for yourself. One for your partner.

D: And one for the world, or somebody who is not physically present.

M: Make a wish for healing for your partner, a wish for healing for yourself, and a wish for healing for someone who's not present, or for the world itself. At your own speed and in your own way acknowledge these three wishes, prayers or intentions now.

D: When you've completed those three intentions, you'll know by the look in your partner's eye that you can gently release your hands. Then go around to as many other people in the room as you can, take their hands, and repeat this process.

Summary of 'The Presence Of Eternity' - Integrating Time Frames

1. Find a partner and stand or sit facing each other, within arms reach.

2. Look at the other person's face and experience yourself in the immediate moment (i.e. be completely aware of what you are seeing, hearing, feeling, tasting and smelling right now - uptime).

3. When you are able to experience yourself as being fully present, reach out your right hand and take the right hand of the person in front of you.

4. Remove your hand, close your eyes, take a deep breath and turn around.

5. Facing your partner again, extend your perception of time from the immediate moment to the context of this activity, to the time frame of the program, to the phase of life that you are in, to your whole life, to a time frame larger than your whole life, extending into your past and future.

6. When you are able to experience a sense of time approaching eternity or timelessness, reach out your left hand and take the left hand of the person in front of you.

7. Remove your hand, close your eyes, take a deep breath and turn around.

8. Face your partner again. Look into each other's eyes and take a breath together, then reach out with both hands and take both hands of your partner.

9. Silently, make three wishes, prayers or intentions for healing: one for yourself, one for your partner, and one for the world or for someone who is not physically present.

Chapter 5

Spiritual Healing

Overview of Chapter 5

- Mercy and Forgiveness
- The Story of the King and Queen
- Unmerited Mercy
- Healing Relationships
- Perceptual Positions
- The Spiritual Healing Process
- Summary of The Spiritual Healing Process
- Basic Elements of Healing

Mercy and Forgiveness

M: It has been said that forgiveness is the most important part of transforming difficult relationships into more loving ones. To "forgive" means to "give as you gave before the hurt occurred." If I want to be born anew, and manifest more of my potential, it's necessary for me to be fresh. And to be fresh, I must heal situations of difficulty that are stopping me. In other words, I must learn how to become more forgiving. This challenge brings with it many questions: "How do I forgive?" "Why forgive anyone in the first place?" "Who deserves to be forgiven?"

Obviously its unreasonable to forgive anybody for anything. Since the rule of the body is to 'survive at any cost', it is not logical to forgive. Therefore, in my view, forgiveness is intimately related to mercy. But what is mercy? Is it compassion? Is it love? What am I doing when I'm being 'merciful'? For me, mercy is "breaking the rules in service of the heart."

The Story of the King and Queen

M: This definition of "mercy" is illustrated in the story of the king and the queen. They each have a big sword and stand in front of their thrones at the top of the stairs in a great hall. They are charged with administering justice for the entire kingdom. The king and queen are duty bound to perform this responsibility without hesitation. One day, the sheriff drags in a man who has stolen some bread, and throws him down on the steps in front of the royal couple. They ask, "What did he do?" The sheriff solemnly replies, "He stole some bread." The king and the queen consult the royal rule book, look at the prisoner and say, "Our book clearly states, 'Steal bread, cut off the head.' That is what we must do. Those are the rules. Now put your head down on that block. We are going to cut it off." As they lift their swords to deliver the lethal blow, the prisoner cries out, "Wait! Please listen to my side of the story. I admit that I did indeed steal the bread. But, I'm a poor man, and my wife and children were hungry. That is why I stole it." Their swords still raised, the king and queen say, "We understand your predicament, but it says right here in the book what we must do. The rule is clear, 'If you steal bread, we cut off your head.' It's there in black and white. That's all there is to it." Looking them in the eye, the prisoner pleads, "Before you strike, put yourself in my shoes. I am like you. Haven't you ever needed something so badly that you broke the rules? My family was starving. I just couldn't stand it anymore." The prisoner's heart felt plea touches the king and the queen. For a moment they are able to see the situation from his perspective. But then an old fear rises within them. Looking at one another, they wonder, "What will happen if we break the rules? What will become of our kingdom? Won't everything fall apart?" Ultimately, however, their compassion is greater than their fear. It has opened them to be deeply touched by the prisoner's humanity. They turn back to him and say, "Even though the rule clearly states that we are supposed to cut off your head, we're going to break the rule in the service of something more important than rules. We will break this rule in service of the heart."

Mercy is the act of breaking the rules in service of the heart. Take a moment and remember when were you last merciful with yourself or with somebody else.

Unmerited Mercy

M: In March of 1966, during the Viet Nam War, I joined the
U.S. Army. As it turned out, I didn't go to Viet Nam —
God was taking care of me in another way. Those of you
who were in Viet Nam, I welcome you home, and thank
you for saving my life. Because if I had gone, I'm fairly
sure I would have come home in a body bag. But I didn't
go there. Instead, I went to Germany and I survived three
years in the Army from '66 to '69. I joined when I was 20
years old and was immediately sent to Fort Ord, which,
until recently, was in Monterey. Monterey is a magnifi-
cently beautiful area on the coast of California. I had been
living in Los Angeles, which might be regarded as a little
less than beautiful sometimes. And one afternoon that
March, the government put me and many other men on a
bus and we drove the long and lonely road to Ft. Ord. I
awoke the next morning and heard countless men screaming and yelling about marching left and right, and I
realized that I was in a situation that I knew nothing
about. It was dangerous and I was frightened.

But I was a young man and I brought poetry books with
me. It was funny — when the bus came into Ft. Ord, we
were on military property and so Army personnel walked
onto the bus. They said, "Okay, if you have any knives
over three inches long, or guns or chains or Playboy
magazines, throw them out here." I was wondering what
they were talking about. I had brought my Lafcadio
Hearn poetry book. But then I heard "Clink! Clink!
Clink!" And several of the young men with me on the bus
were dropping a variety of weapons on the floor. After a
few days of getting oriented to the fort, one morning we
marched to this huge area, the size of 5 football fields. I
stood, facing the magnificent Monterey mountains, among
about a thousand other men with the Pacific Ocean

behind me. The sky above me was clear and blue. The temperature was perfect. All of us were wearing our green fatigues. We each carried a rifle and bayonet. And I was suddenly aware that green fatigues are what men wear when they kill other men in war.

But I didn't want to think of killing. I was thinking of poetry and wondering how I could be in the presence of all of this and somehow maintain my heart. So I stood there looking at the backs of the heads of a thousand men and a thousand rifles, and I wondered how I could be open hearted in the presence of this war machinery.

In the distance I saw a drill sergeant standing on a platform. He held a microphone and he screamed at us to "Stand at attention! Fix bayonets!" And all the time I was wondering and looking at the mountains and the sky. I was doing the best I could to remember where I was.

So, on that beautiful day in Monterey, a thousand young men were standing at attention. And I heard the drill sergeant yell, "Thrust, parry, thrust again." And we acted out the cruel war dance. I remember him screaming a question over and over again to a thousand of us very young men, "What's the spirit of the bayonet?" And, well-prepared, a thousand of us would yell, "To kill! To kill! To kill!" And we would thrust and parry. And it was heart-breaking.

And, in 1966 in the face of Viet Nam, I wondered if I would live to tell the story to anyone.

Twenty one years later, after my experience at Fort Ord, the men and the weapons, after wondering about the the true meaning of the Spirit, I returned to those very mountains. More than a generation had passed. This time, I was in my 40's, and I rented a house on the beach with the woman in my life. We were deeply in love. From the house I would look at the ocean, listen to the pounding surf, and feel the warmth of the fireplace. We were together all night, talking and deeply enjoying each other's company. And in the morning, I got up and decided to go for a run. I put on my jogging shorts and walked outside to the road. As I ran near the ocean, I was very aware of the same Monterey mountains I'd watched while in the Army. The same ocean, the same big sky over it. And I could smell the sea breeze and hear the sea gulls and the pounding surf. As I ran I became gradually aware that I had lived through a time of war. My feelings over-whelmed me. Here I was again, in Monterey, but this time renting a house, and very much in love. I literally felt my heart crack open. I stopped running. There were so many tears I couldn't breathe, and I looked at the ground and at the mountains and the beauty of it. And I got down on my knees and I held sand in my hand and looked closely at it. My tears mixed with the sand.

Suddenly I was struck by the fact that I could feel the sand in my hand, I could taste my tears and I could actually move my hand. I had hands! I was whole. I was not maimed in the war. I was holding sand. And I was so grateful, I could hardly stand it. I cried over the miracle that I could move my hand, that I could taste my tears. And it seemed to me an unspeakably priceless gift. I couldn't possibly explain it to myself or to anyone else. Somehow I was allowed to have this experience, this moment of Grace. I knew that everything was all right and that I belonged. And this belonging, this feeling, was unutterably good and I couldn't possibly have earned it. And in those tears I understood for the first time in my life that Grace is unmerited mercy.

Healing Relationships

M: The dictionary defines "grace" as "unmerited mercy." That is, mercy without justification. Of course, that doesn't make any sense to our rational mind or 'left brain'. It is going to ask, "Why should I be merciful for no reason? I should at least have a reason." Unmerited mercy is not something that makes sense to the conscious mind. But I believe that it does make deep sense to the body. It comes into the body and the heart gets full. To me, the experience of grace is like crying and laughing at the same time. In fact, it is this state of surrender that is most needed to heal situations of difficulty.

But the question still remains, how do we do that?

D: One of the foundations of both the Old and New Testaments of the Bible is to "Love your neighbor as yourself." Regardless of religious preference, I think this is a very deep and important principle of the spirit, and of healing. But again, the question is, "How do you do that?" How do you love your neighbor as yourself, especially if your neighbor is contributing to your difficulties?

Take a moment now and think of a personal relationship that needs to be healed. Identify a relationship with a significant other in which you would like to bring some kind of spiritual healing. It could even be a relationship with a person who is no longer alive, but which still needs some kind of healing.

In our next exercise we are going to explore some answers to the questions we've been asking about how to be more merciful and forgiving. We are going to begin by experiencing several key "perceptual positions" with regard to the relationship you just identified.

Perceptual Positions

Perceptual positions refer to the fundamental points of view you can take concerning a relationship between yourself and another person.

1st Position: Associated in your own point of view, beliefs and assumptions, seeing the external world through your own eyes. Use first person language when talking - "I am seeing," "I feel," etc.

2nd Position: Associated in another person's point of view, beliefs and assumptions, seeing the external world through his or her eyes. Use second person language when talking about your self in first position - "You are", "You look," etc.

3rd Position: Associated in a point of view outside of the relationship between yourself and the other person with the beliefs and assumptions from both 1st and 2nd position. Use third person language when talking about your self in first position or the other person (2nd position) - "He is," "She says," "They are," etc.

D: So "first position" is being in your own body. From this perspective you recognize, "I'm me, you're you, we're not the same."

M: I'm over here and you're over there, and we're different. I am looking out of my own eyes and feeling the world through my own body.

D: If I were to think of my mother, Patricia, from "first position," I would look out at her through my own eyes and see her "over there." I would have my own feelings, and be clear that she is a different person from me. We're not the same.

"Second position" involves putting yourself "into the shoes" of the other person.

M: When you take "second position," it is as if you become the other person for a time.

D: If I were in my mother's shoes, for instance, I'd see "Robert Dilts" over there. I would look at Robert Dilts through Patricia's eyes.

M: Some people say that second position skills are the source of "empathy," "compassion" and "deep understanding". They all come from knowing what it's like to be inside someone else's skin, like the king and queen when they saw the world through the eyes of the prisoner.

D: If I have truly taken "second position" with my mother, then I would take on her posture. I would not be in Robert Dilts' body for the moment. I would be in Patricia's body.

M: "Third position" involves taking an observer perspective. From "third position" you can see both yourself and the other person at the same time. Robert would see himself standing "over there" communicating with Patricia. And as Robert looked at them, he would say, "I see Robert and Patricia talking to one another."

D: From third position, I would not use the words "I" and "you" in describing my interaction with my mother. Rather, I would talk about the interaction using the terms "him," "her" and "them."

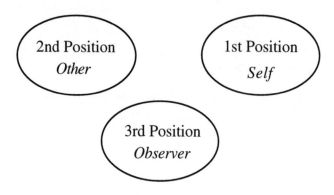

The Three Basic "Perceptual Positions"

The Spiritual Healing Process

D: To create the possibility of using these three perceptual positions as a tool for spiritual healing, Robert and I have added another perceptual position to this basic "trinity." This position is for the state of "spiritual wholeness." The state of "spiritual wholeness" can be used as a resource to transform our experience of a difficult relationship. A tremendous potential for deep healing is created by bringing the experience of the sacred into each perceptual position.

In fact, in our study of various "tools of the spirit," Robert and I noticed that people described several different varieties of spiritual experience. While they were clearly related at some level, at first glance these descriptions appeared to contradict one another. Some people, for instance, described their spiritual experiences as a state in which "everything is an extension of me." In this type of experience, there are no more boundaries between self and others. Rather everything is perceived as being "self."

M: Others, however, described an essentially "egoless" state. Rather than experiencing the world around them as being an "extension of" themselves, they claimed to experience themselves as being "one with" another person, or "one with" the world. It was as if they were so identified with something outside of themselves that their sense of 'self' ceased to exist.

D: A third group, however, described their spiritual experience as a state of feeling "part of" something much larger than the reality they were able to physically perceive.

Initially we were puzzled by the differences between these descriptions of what was presumably the same state. Then we recognized that the experiences of "extension of," "one with" and "part of" are not contradictory, but rather relate to the spiritual expressions of the three basic perceptual positions. To perceive the universe as an "extension of" yourself, is the spiritual expression of 'first position'. To feel "one with" the universe, on the other hand is the spiritual expression of 'second position'. To experience oneself and others as being "part of" something much larger is the spiritual expression of 'third position'.

To me, these states represent three very powerful ways to "love your neighbor as yourself."

First Position + 'Spiritual Wholeness' -> *"The other is an 'extension of' me."*

Second Position + 'Spiritual Wholeness' -> *"I feel 'one with' the other."*

Third Position + 'Spiritual Wholeness' -> *"We are both 'part of' something much larger than us."*

The Spiritual Expression of the Three Basic Perceptual Positions

M: The "Spiritual Healing" process utilizes the position of "spiritual wholeness" to bring healing into a difficult relationship. While it can be done on your own without assistance, the exercise is best done with three people: an "explorer," a "guide," and a "guardian angel."

D: The "explorer" will be moving through the various perceptual positions with respect to a difficult relationship. The 'guide's' job is to direct the 'explorer' and 'guardian angel' to the appropriate positions at the appropriate times. The mission of the 'guardian angel' is to support the explorer as he or she goes through each step, and assist him or her to bring the state of spiritual wholeness into each of the perceptual positions in order to produce transformation and healing.

M: To demonstrate the process, I will be Robert Dilts' 'guardian angel' and accompany him through each step. Before we start, it is important to lay out spaces on the floor for the three basic perceptual positions (self, other and observer) and the state of 'spiritual wholeness'.

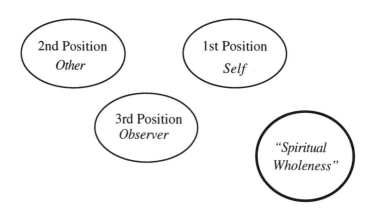

Adding a Location for 'Spiritual Wholeness' to the Three Basic Perceptual Positions

M: Robert begins by putting himself into 'first position' with respect to the relationship in which he is experiencing difficulty, and wants to bring some sort of spiritual healing.

D: (Steps into the 'first position' location.) 'First position' is the place from which I experience the problem. As I stand here, I am imagining that the other person is present and I'm feeling that there's something wrong. You may feel anger or pain, for instance. In the particular relationship that I've chosen to work with, I feel that I'm missing a connection with the other person that I want more of, but which isn't there right now.

M: As the explorer, Robert chooses a situation of difficulty. Whether or not he can clearly articulate the problem he experiences doesn't matter. He simply stands there and accesses that experience, and pays attention to how he feels. He notices how and where he experiences that problem in his body. As he thinks about his relationship with the other person, he imagines the person to be standing in front of him, in the 'second position' location.

D: So I'm imagining the person in front of me and focusing on my own body. I notice where in my body I feel the problem. At this moment, I am feeling a disconnection or barrier between me and the significant other.

M: That's step one. When Robert has done that fully enough to experience his emotional reaction to the situation, he physically steps out of the 'first position' location and shifts his state.

D: (Steps away from the 'first position' location and begins to shake his hands, shoulders and legs.) I like to pretend that the 'first position' location is like a type of "emotional fly paper." Once I've stepped on it, the negative emotions get stuck there, so that I'm free to step away from them and leave them in that location.

M: Once Robert has shifted out of the problem state, I guide him to the 'spiritual wholeness' location. As he physically puts himself in that location, he begins to access the state of 'spiritual wholeness' or connection that he felt at the end of the Sacred Journey process, or during the Presence of Eternity exercise.

D: (Dilts physically steps into the 'spiritual wholeness' location. McDonald moves to his side, standing perpendicular to him.) One of Robert McDonald's duties as my 'guardian angel' is to "anchor" my state of 'spiritual wholeness' so that I will be able to maintain it during the rest of the process. He is going to "anchor" me by gently touching me when I am fully in that state.

M: On one hand, this touch is a bit like Pavlov's bell. It is a stimulus that can be used to help retrigger Robert's experience of 'spiritual wholeness' through associative conditioning. On the other hand, it is something that goes much deeper than that. My touch is also a way of protecting and supporting Robert.

D: Notice that, given the type of experience we are talking about, Robert's touch could actually be a distraction rather than an anchor. If Robert is not in a very deep rapport with me, his touch will most likely disturb my state rather than strengthen it.

M: So, as Robert Dilts enters his state of 'spiritual wholeness', I need to go there with him. As his 'guardian angel', I need to access my own state of 'spiritual wholeness'. Then, when I touch him, it is like the Presence of Eternity exercise. The touch is a signal that we are both in a similar state that creates a space for healing.

D: In order for this work, then, I, as the 'explorer', need to signal my 'guardian angel' that I am in my state of 'spiritual wholeness'. I do this by placing one of my hands over my heart. This is my signal to Robert McDonald that

I am in the state of 'spiritual wholeness' and am ready to be anchored. (Dilts pauses for a moment, then slowly places his hand over his own heart.)

M: Now, as Robert Dilts' 'guardian angel', I do not simply reach out and touch him when I see his hand over his heart. That could be disruptive and a violation of the sacredness of our relationship. I first wait until I am fully in my own state of 'spiritual wholeness'. When I'm ready, I offer my support to Robert rather than force it upon him. I do this by simply putting out my hand, palm up, in front of Robert. When he's ready to have this connection, he takes my hand and places it over his other hand on his heart. (McDonald stands in silence, then offers his hand to Dilts. Dilts takes McDonald's hand and places it over his heart.)

My hand is now over Robert's heart, and his hand is on top of mine. Once he has done this, I move a little closer to him and place my other hand on the upper center of his back. So one hand is covering and protecting his heart, and the other hand is supporting him and 'backing him up'.

D: In addition to his support and protection, another important part of Robert McDonald's mission as my 'guardian angel' is to maintain his own state of 'spiritual wholeness'. And, as he does, Robert can begin to imagine that there is a circle of energy flowing through his arms and intersecting my heart.

M: As I breathe in, I imagine that energy moves from Robert Dilts' heart, up my left arm through my own heart, down my right arm, and back into his heart. I see and feel this circle of energy connecting my heart to Robert's heart. I just keep sending this energy from my right hand, gently through his heart, receiving it in my left hand, and bringing it back up into my heart. The energy is renewed in my heart and through my state. Then I send it down my right arm again and back into Robert's heart, completing the circle. (Dilts and McDonald stand together in silence.)

D: When I am able to be in my own state of 'spiritual wholeness' and feel the contact with my 'guardian angel', then I'm going to return to the 'first position' location. I am going to go back into the experience of the difficult relationship. This time, however, I am taking with me my anchor for 'spiritual wholeness' and my 'guardian angel'. (Dilts steps back to the 'first position' location. McDonald accompanies him, still touching Dilts' heart and upper back.)

M: As Robert Dilts is standing here now, he goes even more deeply into his personal experience of this relationship, bringing with him the resource of 'spiritual wholeness'. As I stand here with him, I continue to maintain my own state of 'spiritual wholeness', feeling my left hand backing him up and my right hand protecting his heart. I also continue to feel the energy that moves through both of our hearts at the same time, with every breath. This gives Robert the chance to perceive this relationship of difficulty in a new way.

D: Even though I am fully in my own body, looking through my own eyes and imagining the other person in front of me as I did before, my experience is very different. It is not that what I'm seeing has changed. Rather, my heart feels like it has melted, instead of being cold. There's more warmth.

M: It is at this point that Robert can begin to expand his sense of 'self' to include the other. His 'first position' can become so large that he can start to notice how this other person is in many ways an "extension of" himself.

D: I begin to experience that the other person is not just a separate individual "out there." Instead, this person is an "extension of" me. This allows me to realize that part of my feeling of disconnection from the person is due to my own fear and guilt of having let that person down in some way. But as I continue to expand myself to include the other person, it is as if our hearts merge together and my entire feeling changes in a way that is difficult to describe in words.

M: So, important transformations occur simply because of the shift in perception brought about by adding the resource of 'spiritual wholeness' to 'first position'. (Dilts and McDonald stand together in silence for a moment.)

When the transformation is completed and the explorer is ready to leave the 'first position' location, he then walks over to the 'second position' location, accompanied by the 'guardian angel'. When he steps into 'second position' the explorer enters into the body experience of the other person in the situation of difficulty. In this case, Robert Dilts will put himself into the shoes of the person from whom he has felt disconnected.

D: (Dilts leaves the 'first position' location and slowly walks over 'second position'. McDonald accompanies him, touching his heart and upper back.)

M: From this perspective Robert sees "himself" over there in the 'first position' location. He feels the internal and emotional experience of the other person, as if he were the other person for a time.

As he does this, however, Robert is also maintaining the state of 'spiritual wholeness', and I continue to protect his heart and support his back as his 'guardian angel'. This allows him to become the other person even more deeply.

D: What happens for me when I bring spiritual wholeness to this position is that, for the first time, I have enough feeling of safety that I can actually put myself into the other person's shoes. One of my first personal realizations is that I've been afraid to go into the shoes of the other person because I might be overwhelmed. With the resource of my state of 'spiritual wholeness' and with Robert McDonald as my 'guardian angel', I'm actually able to put myself into the shoes of that person and start to allow myself to actually feel what it is like to be the other person. What I feel here initially is a lot of pain and fear. But as Robert stays with me and keeps anchoring me and reminding me of my state of 'spiritual wholeness', that fear, and the emotional and physical pain, becomes more tolerable. So the first thing that my "guardian angel's" anchor has helped me to do is to be able to actually get into the shoes of the other person. I wasn't able to do that before. I can now be in the shoes of the other and look at Robert Dilts "over there" through this person's eyes.

M: Now Robert can allow this 'second position' perspective to deepen, and he can become "one with" this other person. He can go to a kind of spiritual extension of 'second position'. As he becomes "one with" this person, he can continue to remain in his state of 'spiritual wholeness' and notice the transformations that naturally occur. (Dilts and McDonald stand together in silence.)

D: There is an emotional melding that happens for me. From inside of this other person, I sense a deep fear of letting "Robert" down. From within the shoes of this person, I'm afraid that, if I have the emotions I am feeling, I've somehow betrayed Robert. And so I'm not able to express myself easily or stay connected with Robert because I'm trying to protect him. He doesn't want me to be afraid or hurt. And he doesn't want me to die.

As I continue to bring the state of 'spiritual wholeness' into this other person's perspective, however, I also realize how deeply the other person loves and trusts Robert. As the other person, I am saying to Robert, "I just want to go home. I just want to go home." And I can see that Robert doesn't really understand what I'm really trying to tell him. But I know that if he could just look into my eyes, past my fear and pain, and into my heart, he would begin to understand that the "home" that I'm talking about is my spiritual home. Then we would both be able to be more at peace.

M: So, from this perspective, Robert gets some very important information about the other person that he didn't have before.

D: And although I used words to describe what I was experiencing, it was primarily an emotional shift that happened in me that is difficult to articulate. I felt like I wanted to cry.

M: And as he maintains his state of 'spiritual wholeness', senses my protection and support, and feels the energy I am sending from my hands to his heart, Robert gets a chance to have a greater healing of that relationship. (Dilts and McDonald again stand together in silence.)

And when Robert has finished this stage of the Spiritual Healing process, he will be ready to move to the 'third position' location.

D: (Leaves the 'second position' location and slowly walks over to 'third position'. McDonald accompanies him, touching his heart and upper back.)

M: From 'third position' Robert observes both "Robert Dilts" and the other person in that situation of difficulty. He watches himself and the other person interact, as if he were a wise and kind observer. At the same time, he maintains his state of 'spiritual wholeness' and continues to sense my presence as his 'guardian angel'. And as he stands here in 'third position' looking at himself and the significant other, he can feel deeply that he's safe enough to watch the relationship from a place of total clarity. Observing them with the knowledge of what it is like to be in each perspective provides him with a greater sense of wisdom.

D: What happens for me here is that I don't see them as two separate entities interacting. From here, I become aware that they have been perceiving each other as fundamentally separate beings that needed to be connected, rather than as fundamentally connected beings.

M: Maintaining the perspective of the wise observer, Robert can continue to allow this 'third position' point of view to expand as he notices that he and the other person are "part of" something much larger.

D: What becomes even clearer from this point of view is that they're actually two parts of the same thing that will always be together. The issues of "disconnection," "let down" or "betrayal" are only meaningful if they start from the belief that they're fundamentally separated.

M: By bringing in his state of 'spiritual wholeness', Robert's 'third position' becomes greatly expanded, and he notices how he and the other person are both "part of" something much larger. This brings with it a profound potential for natural transformation and healing. (Dilts and McDonald stand for a moment in silence.)

D: When I have finished integrating my learnings from this perspective, the last step is for me to walk back to the place of 'spiritual wholeness'. (Dilts leaves the 'third position' location and returns to the 'spiritual wholeness' location accompanied by McDonald.)

M: From here, Robert takes a look at all three of the perceptual positions he has just experienced. He sees them all and feels the transformation that has begun to occur. As he witnesses the healing that is taking place, he allows a symbol or metaphor for that healing to emerge. He allows a symbol or metaphor for that process of healing to emerge into his consciousness, as if it were the birth of something new. It could come in any form. It could be an image, or words or some type of analogy.

D: The image that comes to me is of a walnut. A walnut has two symmetrical parts that are tightly joined together. In order to grow into a tree, however, the two halves must open to allow something new to emerge. When the walnut opens, the shell breaks off of the outside and the plant is free to grow from the meat of the nut. In order for the chute to come out, the shell needs to break open and let the seed that it has been holding fulfill its destiny as a tree. That's the metaphor that comes up for me.

M: Robert can continue to think about this metaphor and how it might be useful in his life now and in the future, in relation to this person. And at a certain moment, Robert will no longer require me to continue to anchor, support, or protect him. He will signal his readiness by releasing my hand which has been over his heart.

D: (Dilts releases McDonald's hand. Both Dilts and McDonald stand in silence for a moment with their hands at their sides.) Thank you Robert. [Applause]

M: Thank you.

Summary of The Spiritual Healing Process

In many respects, the Spiritual Healing process is quite simple. You start from your first person experience of the problem, get out of it, and regain your sense of 'spiritual wholeness'. Your 'guardian angel' also enters the state of 'spiritual wholeness', and together you create a special touch anchor for that shared experience. Then you simply take a walk through each of the three basic perceptual positions, bringing the spiritual resource into each place creating transformation and healing. Finally you return to the state of 'spiritual wholeness' and notice what metaphor for healing emerges.

The specific steps of the process are described below.

1. In the mood of a ceremony, mark out four locations of change on the floor: First, Second and Third Perceptual Position, and a location for Spiritual Wholeness. Let the first three locations of change form a triangle. Place the location for Spiritual Wholeness a few feet away from the triangle.

2. Stand in the First Position Location and remember an interpersonal situation of difficulty in which you want to feel a shift toward Spiritual Wholeness.

3. Step away from the First Position Location and shake-off the experience.

4. Now, stand in the Spiritual Wholeness Location and relive a Wholeness resource state. Physically touch the center of your own heart. At the same time, your 'guardian angel' will access his or her own Wholeness resource state. When you are both fully in the Wholeness state, your 'guardian angel' will also place one hand

over your heart and his or her other hand in the center of your back (thus supporting and backing you up with Wholeness). Your 'guardian angel' will maintain this bodily contact with you throughout the rest of the exercise.

5. Maintaining the state of Spiritual Wholeness, move with your 'guardian angel' and step into the First Position Location. Now, with these additional resources, recall the situation of difficulty from your own perspective. Notice how you feel and how the situation is enriched and transformed by bringing in your Spiritual Wholeness resource state coupled with your "guardian angel's." Now, expand your awareness until you perceive the other person in the situation as an **"extension of"** yourself. Notice how your feelings change.

6. Keeping your hand on your heart, move with your 'guardian angel' into the Second Position Location. With your additional resources, recall the situation of difficulty from the other person's perspective. Notice how you feel and how the situation is enriched and transformed. Deepen your sense of being in Second Position until you sense that you are **"one with"** the other person. Notice how your feelings change.

7. With your hand still touching your heart, move with your 'guardian angel' to the Third Position Location. Now, with these additional resources, see and hear yourself and the other person in the situation of difficulty. Notice how you feel and how the situation is enriched and transformed. Now broaden your sense of being in Third Position until you sense that you and the other person are **"part of"** a much larger and vaster System or 'mind'. Notice how your feelings change.

8. Maintaining the Spiritual Wholeness State, move with your 'guardian angel' and return to the Spiritual Wholeness Location. With the memories of having been in First, Second and Third Position, and with the additional resources, look at all three positions in the situation. Notice what metaphor emerges in your mind, now. That is, what metaphor seems to represent the entire experience you are now witnessing?

9. Share the metaphor with your 'guardian angel', and notice the ways in which your memories of that situation have already changed toward Wholeness and Healing.

Basic Elements of Healing

D: In my study of various healers and the process of wellness, I have found three common components. The process of healing essentially requires:

1. An intention
2. A relationship
3. A ritual

Healing, of course, starts with the 'intention' to heal. With that intention, even the crudest of methods and tools can produce healing. Without it, even the most sophisticated techniques and tools can fail. The intention to heal is most concretely expressed in the relationship between the people involved in the healing context. The depth and intensity required by that relationship is related to the level at which the healing is intended. For instance, healing at the level of body or behavior requires less intensity and depth of relationship than the healing of the mind. Healing which involves one's belief system, identity or spirit places even more emphasis on the quality of the relationship.

The intention to heal and the relationship which supports that intention are manifested through a ritual of some kind. There are many different types of rituals that can be effective. Human history has been filled with a variety of rituals for healing which are all effective in their way. The most important factor in the success of the ritual seems to be its degree of congruence with the level of intention and the relationship it is supporting.

When these three elements are aligned, the deep structures behind healing may be activated and healing occurs in a natural, self-organizing manner. While external techniques and tools may be used mechanically to prod or aid the healing process, the source of healing is within the system of the individual.

In many ways the exercises that we have done so far are fairly simple rituals. Taking hands or walking with somebody into four different locations are not complicated procedures. But, as we pointed out earlier, the procedure is not really where the 'miracle' happens.

First and foremost is the intention for healing. And the intention for healing is different than having it as a goal. You can "fail" at a goal, but not an intention. Intention is an ongoing process. It is more like a prayer than an objective.

Secondly, for that intention to begin to manifest it needs a relationship. For example, in the Spiritual Healing process, the 'explorer' needs a relationship with his or her 'guardian angel'. The 'guardian angel' has an intention for healing, rather than a focus on a specific outcome. The quality of the relationship determines the degree to which the intention for healing can manifest.

The third component is a ritual. A ritual involves a series of actions which symbolize or express the intention and the relationship. Starting with an intention to heal, you enter into a supportive relationship, and bring it into action through the ritual.

This completes our first section on "Birth." And it is traditional in many cultures to celebrate a "birth" with a birthday cake. As part of that celebration you blow out the candles on the cake. Perhaps you can take a nice deep breath, and imagine you are getting ready to blow out a set of candles. Make a wish, and gently release the air from your lungs as if you are blowing out the candles on a birthday cake. Our "birth-day" wish for you is to integrate your learnings thus far, in a way that is most comfortable and appropriate for you.

part two

Death

Opening to the Shadow

Releasing Enmeshment with the Shadow

Self Parenting

Chapter 6

Opening to the Shadow

Overview of Chapter 6

- Letting Go of the Unnecessary
- What Do You Want?
- Changing in the Twinkling of an Eye
- Meaningful and Meaningless Pain
- Robert Dilts' Daughter: Shadows and Light
- Robert McDonald's Father: Loving Anyway
- Opening to the Shadow
- Forms of Enmeshment
- Discovering the Shadow

Letting Go of the Unnecessary

Part I of this book was about "birth" – about new beginnings. This second part is about another area of our experience where we confront issues of a "spiritual" nature. It is about "Death" - in the largest sense of that term. For us, "death" is about 'letting go of that which is no longer necessary'.

What do you want?

M: In the face of death, we get a chance to wake up. This has certainly been true in my life. There have been many deaths in my family, and as a consequence of being around death a lot, I became much more awake. Instead of thinking, "I'm going to live forever," I'm very clear that I am not. So I think, "What am I doing? What's my life about? What's my mission? What's my purpose? I don't have forever in this form."

D: In fact, to begin our exploration of "Death," and to distinguish between that which is necessary and unnecessary, it seems appropriate that we ask a basic NLP question: "What do you want?" In other words, "What brings you to explore *Tools of the Spirit*?" We're sure that there are as many answers to this question as there are readers. Some typical answers we've heard include: "To know my bliss." "To know my path." "To love and have a closer connection to my 'God source'." "To have a better sense of my self-image." "To be able to feel."

M: And, since I define personal identity as "knowing what I feel and what I want," feeling is an essential part of our identity. For example, if right now you are feeling sad, then that is simply what is true for you. The truth of your emotional state is not what 'should be', or 'might be', or is 'supposed to be'. Rather it is simply your authentic experience. This is important because many people believe, "If I'm going to be 'Spiritual,' then surely I won't have any sad feelings. It'll be cotton candy on Sunday morning. If I'm going to be with God, surely I won't have my heart broken. If I walk with Christ, if I talk with Krishna and the Virgin Mary, hang out with Abraham . . . if I have an experience of Buddha-nature, if I'm a bodhisattva, if I'm enlightened, well surely there is no sadness in that." Saints don't cry, of course. Or do they?

D: Some other answers Robert and I have heard in response to this basic NLP question are: "To remember that I'm always safe." "To experience openness." "To integrate my professional and personal lives." "To know that I'm not alone." "To know that I am part of God." "To know that God is part of me." "To be aware that home is everywhere."

M: It seems to me that God is aptly defined by Capra, Stendl and Thomas, in *Belonging To The Universe*, as "That to which we ultimately belong and which ultimately belongs to us." One of the goals of *Tools of the Spirit* is to help us know that we belong.

D: I think that in many ways we all want to belong, to love, to be safe, to feel joy, peace, and much more. This exploration of "Death" is about what stops us from having or experiencing what we are calling 'universally valued' outcomes. What gets in the way of having what we want?

Changing in the Twinkling of an Eye

M: Thinking about what prevents us from having what we want in life, reminds me of an experience I had in Santa Cruz. About two years ago, my friend Danae and I drove into town to see Bernie Siegel, the famous medical doctor and author who works with his patients at the level of transformation. I was very excited to hear whatever he had to say, so we arrived at the auditorium a full half-hour early. The place was empty. After we walked in and looked around, I decided to sit in the perfect spot, about 5 rows back from the stage, in the middle of the room. Dr. Siegel would soon be lecturing directly in front of me, and that was exactly what I wanted. Danae sat down next to me. And, as she placed her coat on the chair to her right, she said, "My friend Alice will be here soon so I am saving a chair for her." After a few minutes, a lot of people arrived. Then Danae said, "Oh, I forgot. There are two more people who are coming." So she saved two more seats. At this point, then, Danae was seated to my right, then there was Alice's empty chair, and then there are two more empty seats.

As the auditorium started to fill up I leaned over and said to Danae, "I'm going to get some apple juice and I'll be back in a minute." I walked into the lobby, got the apple juice and visited the bathroom. But when I returned to the auditorium, I saw a strange woman sitting in my chair, the chair I'd just spent a half an hour saving. Next to her was this large, broad-shouldered young man. Next to him was Alice, and then Danae. Five chairs to the right of where I had been sitting was an empty seat waiting for me ... and there was a woman with tall hair sitting in front of that empty chair. Feeling disappointed, I sat down in the chair and looked at the hair of the woman in front of me. In my new seat I could barely see where Bernie Siegal would be standing. I looked to my left, toward the center seat, and I saw Danae next to me, then Alice, then a big guy, and then a woman sitting in <u>my</u> seat.

I thought, "That's okay, I'm an NLP trainer, no problem! I'll just create a positive anchor and I'll shift my state; it'll be just fine." So I did swish patterns, talked to myself and reanchored myself. But I was still upset. There I was, trying to be spiritual and failing miserably.

And Bernie's going to come in any minute now. So I asked Danae if she would come with me for a second. I wanted to talk to her because I couldn't understand how she managed to allow someone to sit in my special seat while I was getting apple juice. We walked outside and I said, "Danae, I feel a little embarrassed and kind of ashamed of myself that this bothers me at all, but it does." I was upset. I said, "Who are these people? And why is *that* woman sitting in *my* seat?" And Danae said, "Oh, I thought you knew. That big guy is Alice's brother-in-law. Alice's sister is sitting in your seat. She wanted very much to see Bernie Siegal up close. She's hoping to have a new understanding or healing experience here. She has cancer." I felt an instant change in me. Immediately I knew that my new chair was the right one for me. My emotional upset vanished. I was perfectly happy. It occurred to me at that moment that spiritual transformation can happen in the twinkling of an eye.

D: There is another lesson in Robert's story which relates to what we call the *"Shadow."* Very often when we want to be spiritual and open our hearts more fully, somebody comes along and sits in the chair that we have been saving for half an hour.

M: Or a decade. Or a whole life time. And then, perhaps, a "Shadow" emerges.

D: In *Tools of the Spirit*, we define the Shadow as some aspect of ourselves that we have turned away from, denied, repressed, and tried to get rid of. A part of ourselves that we are unable to love, unable to cherish, unable to give a proper place in our lives. The Shadow is the thing that makes us embarrassed. It is the thing that we do not want to feel, that we do not want to have. But we cannot make it go away. In this way, the "Shadow" is our personal reaction to something in ourselves that we don't want to face.

Meaningful and Meaningless Pain

M: There is a story of a man who traveled many miles and
endured much hardship to see a famous therapist. When
the man finally arrived at the therapist's office, he was
obviously in great pain. He told the therapist that he
desperately needed her help. The therapist, who may
have been an NLP practitioner, naturally asked, "What do
you want?"

The man said, "I've heard about you for years. You are
an expert in your field. Please make my hand stop hurting."

The therapist, being exceptionally alert, had noticed from
the beginning that the man had placed his hand on a hot
stove. So she mustered a knowing authority in her voice and
said, "You have your hand on a hot stove."

The man said, "Yes, I know. Please make my hand stop
hurting."

The therapist cleared her throat and said, "If you'll just
remove your hand from the hot stove, it will stop hurting."

The man said, "But you don't understand, I don't want
to remove my hand. I just want you to make my hand
stop hurting."

Thinking it over, the therapist said, "So, you don't want
to change your behavior. You just want your hand to stop
hurting. Well, it is possible through a variety of methods,
including surgically severing your nerves, to remove all
feeling from your hand. However, if you keep your hand
on the hot stove, even though the pain is gone, your hand
will certainly be destroyed. Perhaps it's time for you to
respectfully listen to your pain. It is obviously telling you
something of vital importance."

In this allegory, the man wants to end his pain. He
finds no value in it. And since he can see and feel the
stove burning his hand, he knows something about the
source of his pain. But this insight is not enough. He
wants to do what he has always done and not experience

the natural consequences of his behavior. He doesn't know, yet, how to learn from his suffering. He doesn't know that all pain has 'message value'.

How many of us ignore the messages of our bodies and emotions? When we superficialize our pain, we miss the opportunity to better understand ourselves. We ignore our deepest feelings and highest goals. Then, like the man with his hand on the hot stove, if we do not learn from our pain, if we do not honor the positive purpose of our suffering, we may demand a solution which is not only unhealthy but ultimately the source of even more damage.

The man, whose hand hurt so terribly, could only focus on the goal of ending the pain. He didn't realize that some people would do anything for the ability to feel pain. Leprosy, for example, destroys certain nerves in a person's extremities, so no pain is felt in the finger-tips. Consequently, parts of fingers can be torn off without the leper feeling anything. Long ago, when many lepers were forced to live in caves, the rest of the population thought that the disease destroyed fingers. Actually, while the lepers slept, cave-dwelling rats would eat their fingers. And the lepers did not have the blessing or gift of pain to signal the need to quickly move their hands out of danger.

It is possible to use our personal suffering as a guiding light to illuminate its source and essential structure. Pain has message value because it tells us where to look, and where to tenderly and compassionately attend to our wounds. The pain guides us to the source of the wound. The pain usually whispers at first, but when ignored, it can scream for our attention.

At another level, the overarching gift of our emotional discomfort is compassion for another person's pain. Our suffering can bring human beings together in mutual understanding. When we suffer, we often seek the company of others. Our pain humbles us. It is the great equalizer. Like birth, disease, old age and death, pain ignores our arrogance and brings us to our knees, where somehow we are all the same height. In other words, if my life were totally pain-free, if I had never suffered in any way, I would be unable to commiserate with other people, unable to understand or identify with them. The suffering I experienced as a child in an emotionally shattered, alcoholic family brought me the opportunity for spiritual depth and greater compassion for others. Without my own skinned knee, without my own pains from the past and the present, how would I come to truly know the value of the Golden Rule? I suffer, and so I know you in ways I cannot articulate.

It seems to me that the suffering I've endured in my life has been necessary to deepen my partnership with the human community and to humble me in the face of that which I cannot consciously control. From this perspective, the profound gift or jewel of the pain is compassion. The Latin roots of 'compassion' are *com* which means 'with' and *passion* which means 'to suffer.' Compassion, therefore, means 'to suffer with.' When we feel compassion for someone, we are aware that the other person's suffering reflects our own pain and, in a larger sense, the human condition. In this way, compassion may be seen as the basis of civilization. We are more likely to be civil when we are aware of our own pain and can imagine ourselves in the shoes of other people. Perhaps compassion and the kindness it engenders are also the basis for creating a world to which people will truly want to belong.

D: The therapist said to the man who had his hand on the hot stove, "Remove your hand from the stove; it's causing you pain," and the man said, "No. I want *you* to stop my pain." In a way, this trivializes his pain. And the definitions that Robert McDonald provides, in his Emotional and Spiritual Vocabulary in the appendix, specifically distinguish between "pain" and "hurt." In our way of talking about it, "pain" is a physical sensation. "Hurt," however, is an emotional reaction to pain that has no meaning. For example, when my young son falls down on his bicycle and scrapes his knee, he feels pain; but it doesn't bother him. This is because his pain has meaning. In fact, he is often proud of his scrapes. He might show them off to his friends as a "red badge of courage."

It is much more difficult to deal with "hurt", which is "meaningless pain". When pain has meaning it is much more manageable.

Consider the experience of childbirth. When my wife was in labor with our children, she experienced a lot of "pain," but not "hurt". As her birthing coach, I did more than simply tell her to breathe. It was very important to her that I remind her of the meaning of what she was going through - that she was giving birth to a child that she would love and cherish. When she was able to stay in touch with the meaning, the labor didn't "hurt," even though there was still significant physical pain.

I do not say this in order to trivialize her pain, nor to suggest that we need to seek out painful experiences in order to learn or to grow. Rather, it is important to distinguish between "meaningful" and "meaningless" pain. We do not want people to go through unnecessary or meaningless pain. In fact, a primary reason that both Robert and I got into NLP was because we realized that it was possible to alleviate unnecessary suffering. One of the most wonderful things about NLP is that it provides so many tools to help alleviate suffering. That's one of the reasons why we do *Tools of the Spirit*.

On the other hand, to anesthetize people to pain that they need to feel robs them of important learnings. Many people think of painful feelings as simply being "bad." As soon as they have any kind of negative emotional response, they try to dissociate from it. But dissociating can also take away the possibility of finding the value and meaning of the pain.

Meaningful and Meaningless Pain

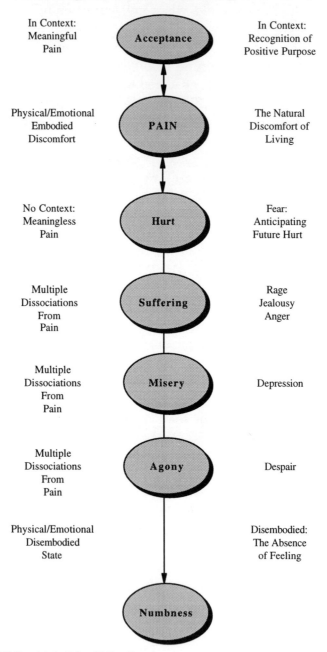

In Context:
Meaningful
Pain

Acceptance

In Context:
Recognition of
Positive Purpose

Physical/Emotional
Embodied
Discomfort

PAIN

The Natural
Discomfort of
Living

No Context:
Meaningless
Pain

Hurt

Fear:
Anticipating
Future Hurt

Multiple
Dissociations
From
Pain

Suffering

Rage
Jealousy
Anger

Multiple
Dissociations
From
Pain

Misery

Depression

Multiple
Dissociations
From
Pain

Agony

Despair

Physical/Emotional
Disembodied
State

Disembodied:
The Absence
of Feeling

Numbness

M: Here is a model I developed which describes various
reactions to pain.   If someone hits my arm, I will feel
pain.   This pain is the natural discomfort of living in
"duality."   But, if I am unable to recognize the positive
function of the pain, and am unable to discover a context
for the pain which will make it meaningful, then it's as
though I step away from the actual pain.   And instead of
simple pain, I feel **hurt** *about* the pain.   That is, if the
actual pain doesn't make any sense to me, I feel hurt.   I
begin to wonder, "Why did I get hit?   Why do I have this
pain?"   In other words, if I find no meaning in the pain, I
might separate from the pain and feel hurt about the
pain.   'Hurt' is the word I use to describe the experience of
meaningless pain.

Now if I continue to move away from my meaningless
pain, if I step farther away from the actual pain and even
away from my hurt, then I feel **angry** about the hurt over
being hit on the arm.   And this anger is a form of
suffering, a result of multiple dissociations from pain.
That is, I'm suffering over the hurt about being hit on the
arm.

Now, if I step away from the anger and even farther
away from my original pain, then I can feel **depressed**.
And this depression is a form of **misery**.   That is, I'm
miserably depressed about the fact that I am suffering,
because I'm hurt about the pain in my arm.

And then if I step even farther away from my original
pain, I enter **agony**.   I'm agonizingly in **despair**.   And
eventually I can step so far away from my initial experience that I am **numb**.

The schematic on the previous page illustrates what
happens when we move away from our pain.   In my view,
multiple dissociations from simple pain are what many of
us seem to think will bring safety and peace; however, the
reality is precisely the opposite: <u>multiple dissociations
from meaningless pain ultimately bring us to numbness</u>.

Unfortunately, it seems that many of us confuse disembodied numbness with the goal of profound spiritual bliss. And this numbness, this disembodied state is not a state of spiritual happiness or oneness. It is simply the state of non-feeling. But, if I come back into my body, I can feel my pain and notice where and how much pain I feel. Then simple pain is the natural discomfort of being alive.

Perhaps the most important question about pain is, "How should I best regard it?" Or, "How can I find meaning in it?" Of course, when we move from psychology to spirituality, we leave the entire realm of skills and good and bad feelings, and enter a realm where we might paraphrase a question from *A Lazy Man's Guide to Enlightenment* by Thaddeus Golas: "What did I think it was that needed my loving kindness?" Did I think it was happy walks on Sunday? In Tools of the Spirit we're saying that what needs your loving kindness is your "Shadow." What needs your greatest open-hearted sweetness, what needs your kisses and your embrace is simple pain itself.

This may seem to make no rational sense. The "rational" response to pain is to avoid it or dissociate from it, as the schematic indicates. But the "Spiritual" answer is to transcend and embrace it - to love anyway that which we fear. In this way, our greatest fear becomes our guide to love. Let me put it another way: If you love Hell, you're in Heaven. If I love Hell, and I don't mean like Hell, but find the beauty in it, if I open my heart to that which is most heartbreaking, I can be in Heaven.

However, our typical response is to move away from pain. The Spiritual response is to notice that that which hurts the most guides us to what needs to be integrated. It points the way. It's the path. Whatever is in the way, *is* the way. If I come home to my body, I am in a position to find out what I'm feeling and what I'm most afraid of, and what it all means to me. In this way, hurt, anger, suffering depression, misery, agony, despair and numbness can be transformed.

The Spiritual perspective provides the meaning which allows us to experience our pain as simply pain. I can fight my experience or I can open myself and accept what I feel, including my pain, as useful and worthy of my love. It seems to me that the Spiritual perspective reminds us to surrender to something greater than ourselves. Perhaps the ultimate state is the love of life and death, the Light and the Shadow.

D: Some people hear that and think, "How can you put together the acceptance of suffering and 'creating a world to which people want to belong'?" It is important to remember, however, that we are not talking about accepting "unnecessary" suffering. But, if we're afraid to experience pain, it is impossible to know what is "necessary" and what is "unnecessary." For me, the acceptance of my pain allows me to respond to it more wisely.

M: Acceptance leads to the wisdom to look beyond our suffering to discover its meaning. Necessary pain has a message to deliver. For example, one of my clients had psoriasis. I told him, "Go inside and ask the part of you that created the psoriasis for its positive purpose. What message does it have for you?" The part that created the psoriasis responded, "I really want to give you a chance to get some distance from people. You need to have more alone time, to be more at peace." In this case, the positive purpose of the psoriasis was peace of mind. The indication of the need for peace of mind, of course, was the psoriasis which my client initially experienced as "meaningless" pain. But he needed more alone time, more peace of mind, more meditative, contemplative times. That was the message of his physical symptoms. It was also a gift. It reached consciousness through the form of the psoriasis. Once the message was delivered the pain became almost unnecessary because he had received the gift of the message. What made it fully unnecessary was having the tools to change it.

So, pain becomes "unnecessary" once 1) it has delivered its gift or message, and 2) we possess the tools to transform it. Pain *is* necessary when it has not delivered it's gift, and continues to try to deliver its gift, but the person remains unable to make sense of it. My client initially thought, "This is meaningless. Why should I have this terrible bodily disease? It makes no sense." He had not yet discovered its meaning. In other words, if a person doesn't receive the message of his or her symptom, it's still necessary pain. If he or she gets the message but is unable to end the pain, it's also "necessary" pain because it can't be changed.

Here's another example. Let's say you have a fear of public speaking. If you uncover the positive purposes behind your fear, and also learn effective methods to transform that fear into excitement and improved self-esteem, then your upsetting emotional reactions are fully resolvable, and therefore no longer "necessary." On the other hand, if you have no way to transform your fear, and you haven't discovered its deeply personal message-value or gift, then your suffering will continue unabated. "Necessary" suffering is that suffering which we are unable to control <u>and</u> which continues to hold an undelivered gift.

D: "Meaning" then is a major factor determining whether pain is necessary or unnecessary. In Robert's story about the woman who sat in his chair at Dr. Siegel's talk, a single piece of information transformed his feelings. The knowledge that the woman had cancer, put the situation in a context that gave it profound meaning. One of the values of Spiritual awareness is that it provides a context large enough to contain and give meaning to all of our experiences, even the most traumatic.

M: In a surprising way, my father's suicide was one of the greatest gifts he ever gave me. Of course, I couldn't say that at the time. The overwhelming grief typically felt by survivors of suicide is an extraordinary pain because of the trauma, helplessness, guilt, shame and anger. But out of the depths of my suffering came the jewel of a deeper compassion. I am convinced that there is a jewel in every pain. And perhaps one jewel of deep emotional suffering is the love I have for life even when I know that life includes pain and death.

D: The purpose of our activities relating to "Death" are to help answer the questions, "How to we get and give meaning to that which is meaningless? How do we accept that which is necessary, and let go of that which is no longer necessary? How do we face our own Shadows?"

M: In order to accomplish this, we need each other's tenderness, compassion, and deep understanding of our discomfort. We need to feel loved in "every most hidden part" of ourselves. We need the qualities and values of the Heart.

Robert Dilts' Daughter: Shadows and Light

D: Our Shadow is a part of ourselves that may embarrass us. It's the part that we don't want to feel or even admit is a part of us. But we can't make it go away. In fact, I like to point out that the brighter the light, the darker the shadows. When I have had even a minor spiritual awakening, I suddenly see shadows that I didn't see before because the light has gotten brighter.

When my daughter was born, for example, it was one of the most wonderful experiences of my life. I think it is transformational for a man to have a daughter. When Julia was born, parts of my heart opened that I didn't even know were there before. She was a really bright light. But after spending the whole summer with her, I had to travel again. I flew to Europe to do a seminar. It was the first time I was very far away from her. One morning I was in the bathroom at my hotel getting ready to go to the seminar. I had the television on, and I heard crying in the other room. For a moment, I thought it was my daughter crying out in pain or fear. I hurried to the other room and found that the cry was coming from the television. They were showing reports of people in Somalia. On the screen was a baby girl in Mogadishu who was dying of starvation.   Her cry sounded just like my daughter's. I was so connected to my daughter, it was as if my heart was being broken by the image on television. Before Julia had been born, I would have just seen an anonymous image on television. Now the suffering of a child thousands of miles away was breaking my heart.

I realized in that moment that I had a choice: I could close down and say, "Oh this is something that is happening very far away from me. It is happening to somebody very different from me, that I don't even know or care about." Or, I could keep my heart open and realize that the baby was no farther away than my own daughter (both physically and emotionally). The specter of suffering and death became a very real Shadow. The fact that people were dying of starvation wasn't something I could just think of as a concept any longer. I was feeling it. And to choose to close my heart would have meant to somehow love my daughter less. I realized that to love my daughter meant that I had to allow my heart to be broken. It was as if someone that I loved was dying and I was helpless to do anything about it. That Shadow had been there all my life, but the darkness and reality of it had never before been so obvious.

This is an illustration of how, when the light gets brighter, the Shadow becomes more visible. In the presence of the light, we can no longer ignore pain, suffering and fear.

A basic message for the Death theme is that the way to transform or deal with our Shadows, is to 'love anyway'. For me that was the decision that I made with respect to the starving baby and my daughter. I decided to 'love anyway', which meant loving the little girl who I saw dying on television, even if I was helpless, and could do nothing about it, even if loving her led to greater pain in my life.

Robert McDonald's Father: Loving Anyway

M: The more you are aware of what you love, the more likelihood there is for a broken heart. Psychologically speaking, one of the reasons we avoid admitting what we want, and lie about it to ourselves and others, is that, if we know what we want, we might not get it. Our positive intention in this case is to experience inner peace, but instead we become less alive, and more numb. We believe that if we just stay kind of dead, then we won't have to experience the painful aspects of life. And this brings us to the central question when we work with our Shadows, "What do we do with the Shadow?" We know Christ talked about loving our enemies. But how do we love our Shadows? Another question is, "Why would I do that? Why would I love in the face of pain and heartbreak? Isn't there a way for me to love and not get my heart broken?"

When I was 40 years old my mother told me that the man I thought was my father might not be my father. That was quite a shock to me. The man I always thought was my father, Bill McDonald, committed suicide when I was 27. He came from a hard drinking family, was an alcoholic and killed himself on Christmas Day, 1972. So when my mother said, "He might not have been your father," this had a profound impact on every aspect of my life. If Bill McDonald wasn't my father then maybe my biological father didn't commit suicide, and if that were true, maybe I had a completely different ancestry. That could explain one heck of a lot about my life. The uncertainty about who fathered me was a major family secret. When all this was happening to me, I wondered if there were any families without family secrets.

My mother said, "I wanted you to know because I very much loved the other man. When I was pregnant with you we weren't sure whether or not you were his or Bill McDonald's." In my opinion my mother was being very courageous. I am very proud of her because she shared with me something deeply important to her which she could have continued to keep a secret. And if she had died with that secret untold, my life would have been very different. I feel very honored that she would share such sensitive and important information with me.

Because of my mother's courage, I was able to search for my father. I thought if I could find the other man, I could find a way to determine if he was my biological father. I hired somebody to look for him. I examined some old photographs and, interestingly enough, the two men looked a lot alike.

Eventually I discovered that the other man had died about 6 years earlier. I wasn't sure whether or not my biological father died 6 years earlier or had committed suicide 13 years earlier. How could I know who my father was? I tried but I couldn't solve the puzzle. Eventually I simply surrendered.

Very soon after giving up my fruitless search, I had a dream that Bill McDonald came to visit me. And in my dream he stood right beside me. I was seated, he was standing. He looked at me and put his left hand out for me to see. I looked at it for a moment and then put my left hand out and we both looked at our left hands. In a matter-of-fact tone, he said, "You see?" And, shrugging my shoulders, I said, "Yeah, that's your left hand and this is mine." And then he moved his thumb in a special way, and I noticed the double joint at the base of his left thumb. I said, "Yeah, I have a double joint there too, and I can do that. I remember you showed me that when I was a little boy because this is how we know....". I looked at him and almost shouted, "You're my father!" All at once I knew. He had come to me in the dream to tell me that he was my father. I wept.

He said, "Yes." Then he walked away and leaned back on a couch. I looked at my hand and I felt this over-whelming feeling of coming home, of knowing him, of finding my father. And I stood up, and started to walk toward him. I felt my arms opening because my heart was so full; it had just burst open and I was so absolutely vulnerable, waiting to embrace him. "You're my dad, my father. Here you are, my father." Just as I was getting close to him, my arms wide open, I was struck with the realization that he was going to die, that he would commit suicide. If I kept my arms open, if I kept loving him, my heart would be totally broken. At that moment, I knew I had a choice. And that choice was brilliantly clear to me. I could either close down and not love at all, or I could continue to open. I could continue to love. But if I continued to love my heart would surely be broken.

At that moment, I realized there was no other choice, because no other choice made sense. There was only one thing to do and that was to love anyway, even in the face of pain and heartbreak and overwhelm. There was noth-ing else to do because if my heart closed, life wasn't worth living. With a closed heart there is no possibility of joy, no possibility of being fully alive. So I kept my heart open and loved him anyway. And my heart has been broken, and has healed.

My father taught me that love is 100% participation in life, knowing that who you love will be taken from you;

knowing that if you love, your heart will be broken. Love is fully participating knowing that everything you hold dear is changing, is impermanent and will die. The room you are in will fall apart. Our bodies are falling apart. Everything will die. And right now, we are dying. I love Robert Dilts. One day he'll die. I'll die. Yet, that is no reason to withhold love. 'Loving anyway' is what my father taught me that night. And yet if we love anyway, our hearts will be broken. It is not a guess. It's a guarantee. And the question is, "What's the value of continuing to love anyway? What's the value of continuing to open again and open again and open again?" And what's the alternative?

Opening To The Shadow

D: One of our explorations for today is, "What prevents us from letting go of that which is no longer necessary in order to recover that which is so deeply important to us?"

M: What we want is clear. We want Fruits of the Spirit, such as peace, joy, self-love, or a "closer walk with God." What stops us from having them right now? What could possibly stop us from having God's presence or deep inner peace or joy in our lives right now?

D: Whatever stops you right now is what we would call the "Shadow".

M: Most of us perceive the Shadow as something to get rid of, to destroy, or to attack. We find fault with our Shadows instead of noticing that they bring us to our knees, a posture often associated with transformation.

D: One of our processes is called <u>Opening to the Shadow</u>. It is a way of directly experiencing your own Shadow.

M: This exercise requires a certain amount of space. To do it, you may want to take your shoes off and stand in the center of the room. If you're wearing glasses, put them somewhere where they'll be safe. This process requires access to feelings, or first position, to be emotionally embodied.

D: In this exercise, you will be making use of two physical locations. One location is for a "first position" or self position, the other is for a "third position" or observer position. Create these locations by marking out two places on the floor, one in front of the other. The one in front is the self position. You will go through most of the exercise while standing in this location. Near the end of this exercise we will ask you to take a step backward into the observer position.

To begin the exercise, step into your "self position." While standing in the self position, remember the image, symbol, or metaphor, that you created for your large "S" Self. This is the Self that you want to be. It includes the sense of spiritual wholeness and spiritual connection that you desire more of. It contains the sense of healing, love, deep inner peace, joy, safety, connectedness and belonging.

M: Feeling how much you want these Fruits of the Spirit, please say out loud, *"Love is totally participating in the face of change, impermanence and death."* Let yourself feel what these words mean. And as you allow your feelings to deepen within you, you can also think about God or Spirit or Source.

D: Feeling your sense of connectedness with God, Spirit or Source, say aloud, *"I've stopped trying to change you, Spirit, or God. I now intend to understand and accept myself as I am."*

Notice what these words mean for you inside.

M: Become aware of how many times you've tried to change God. How often you've worked hard to make God's Will, or the Universe, be something other than it is? How often have you insisted that you know the right way and that God's "a little behind?"

D: Perhaps you have found yourself saying, "If only God were more compassionate... If only God were more wise or loving... If only God were more caring, then the world would be more to my liking."

M: Perhaps, in the past, you have argued that if God were more loving or aware, then there wouldn't be any suffering in places like Mogadishu or Bosnia. But now, in this exercise, you're declaring, "I've stopped trying to change you, God. I intend to accept myself as I am."

Get a feeling for this decision. And as you stand in the center of the room, begin to open your arms very wide. It's as though you're opening to God, Spirit, Christ, Buddha, the Virgin, Source, Universe, or the One Song. You're opening to whatever God wants. You're saying out loud, *"I give myself to you, (God, Christ, Spirit, Source). I give myself to you ... no matter what."* Even if you want to have the world the way it is. Even if you want to kill my children.

D: What feeling would you have if God wanted to take away everything that is most valuable and precious for you?

M: Even if opening to God means that your heart will be broken completely, say, "I will do whatever You want; I'm giving myself to You, fully."

D: As you say this, notice in your body what Shadow begins to emerge. What stops you from being totally open?

M: Notice what stops you from surrendering completely to God now. What pains, what thoughts, what confusions stop you?

D: And notice where you feel this reaction, this negative or limiting painful reaction, in your body. Where do you feel this Shadow? Where does it live in your body?

M: Where do you feel the fear or the resistance in your body? Touch the part of your body where you feel your reaction to the Shadow. Let this feeling become more intense.

D: Intensify this feeling. Rather than avoid it, allow your attention to focus fully on the Shadow for a moment. Be with it.

Feel the Shadow in your body. Touch that part of your body and allow an image or a symbol that represents this Shadow to begin to emerge.

M: You might see or feel a knife, a weapon, a coffin or even the presence of another person. The Shadow might even take the form of a vague shape or an abstract symbol.

What is your representation of this Shadow which causes you to experience fear, hurt, or anguish? If you don't see an image or a symbol, simply reach out and allow your hands to sculpt it. Allow your hands to sculpt whatever is in your way. Let your hands sculpt a representation of the source of your fear, trauma or hurt.

D: Trace an outline with your hands. Let yourself be in this emotional state for a while and really notice the shape of whatever is causing your reaction.

M: When you have identified your symbol or image for the Shadow, gently take one step back to the observer position, so that you can see yourself in front of you.

D: Disassociate from your experience of the Shadow and shift your physiology.

M: In front of you, see yourself connected to the Shadow. See yourself and the Shadow, and see how the two are connected, how they are enmeshed with each other. Point to the image of yourself and the Shadow in front of you, and say, "There is myself and there's the Shadow." See how they are connected or enmeshed.

Forms of Enmeshment

M: An "enmeshment" with a Shadow is made up of the three parts: (1) the Shadow itself, (2) the form of attachment, and (3) yourself.

There are as many forms of attachment as there are people. A typical form of attachment, for example, is a cord connecting yourself with the Shadow. The representation of the Shadow itself could take the form of a serpent coiled around you, or it may be an anchor attached to your hip; a dagger in your heart; a sword extending down your throat; a black eel-like animal inhabiting your body; barbed wire embedded in your brain; etc. My own Shadow emerged as a pool of black ink that was touching my body and staining it black.

D: My Shadow was like a mass of black strings that entered my body through my throat.

M: When you have identified your Shadow and the form of attachment, take another step backward and brush off your body. Use your hands to flick off any disturbing energy.

D: Our next step will be to do a process that is based on a format that Robert McDonald initially developed for working with addictions and co-dependency (see *Heart of the Mind*, 1989, *Homecoming*, 1990). It is called Releasing Enmeshment with the Shadow.

The following is a summary of what we have done so far.

Discovering The Shadow
(The Archetype Patterns)

The Shadow can be thought of as an archetype that seems to keep you away from Spirit, or Freedom, or the Source, or Oneness, or Wholeness, or God. To find your personal experience of the Shadow, say aloud:

Love is totally participating in the face of change, impermanence and death.

"I've stopped trying to change You (Spirit, Wholeness, Source, God, etc.). I now intend to understand and accept myself as I am."

1. Stand with your arms wide open, speak aloud and say, "I give myself to You (Spirit, Wholeness, Source, etc.), *no matter what.*" The key is in the words, "No matter what."

2. After saying "no matter what", notice any 'Shadow' that emerges. For example, fear, aloneness, death, past pain, trauma, anticipated pain, etc.

3. Where in your body do you feel a connection or reaction to the Shadow?

4. Touch the part of your body where you feel a reaction to the Shadow.

5. Now allow an image or symbol to come to your mind. This image or symbol represents the Shadow. For example, you might see an object like a knife, medieval weapon or a coffin; or you might see a person whom you recognize or do not recognize; the shadow might even be a vague shape. Just notice what comes to your mind. Even if you don't see an image or symbol, simply reach out and allow your hands to intuitively trace the outlines of it.

6. Now, take a moment to step back into an observer position in which you can see a) your Shadow, b) the way in which you are attached to the Shadow, and c) yourself.

Chapter 7

Releasing Enmeshment with the Shadow

Overview of Chapter 7

- **Robert Dilts' Shadow Work**
- **Summary of the Releasing Enmeshment With the Shadow Process**
- **Discussion of the Releasing Enmeshment Process**
- **Releasing Enmeshment as a Path to Spiritual Growth**
- **Robert McDonald's Shadow Work**
- **The Emperor's Looking Glass**
- **Saying Good-Bye**
- **The Monk and the Tiger**

Robert Dilts' Shadow Work

M: We are going to demonstrate the <u>Releasing Enmeshment with the Shadow</u> process, with Robert Dilts as the 'explorer'. To begin, Robert will need to return to the 'self position' location and re-experience his Shadow attachment.

D: So, I am going to step forward from my observer position back into my first person position. (Dilts steps from 'observer' location to 'self position'.)

M: And while standing in the first position location, Robert, please bring the sense of your Shadow back into your body.

D: The Shadow that I experience is something that gets in my way of being congruent. It relates to my voice, and the ability to speak my truth. I physically feel it as dark tendrils that enter my body through my throat.

Exploring the Structure of the Shadow

M: Take your time to fully retrieve your feeling of attachment to your Shadow. As you sense the attachment to the Shadow in your body, imagine you have "magical hands" which you can use to explore this attachment within your body. Imagine feeling the attachment with your hands now, and notice how deeply these tendrils penetrate your body. Where do they go? (Dilts moves his hands as if touching and sculpting invisible threads.)

D: They go down into my heart.

M: Do they go any deeper than your heart, or just to your heart? (Dilts continues to move his hands, as if touching something invisible on his body.)

D: They go around and inside my heart.

M: Around and inside. How high do they go up? (Dilts continues to feel around with his hands, touching different areas of his body.)

D: They go various places. One group of strands goes to my brain and my head.

M: Continue to use your "magical hands" to explore this attachment. Find out where these strands enter your body. Then follow them from the entrance and discover where they are coming from. (Dilts touches his throat, and then begins to move his hands away from his body, as if feeling something in front of him.)

Let your hands physically sculpt the path of the tendrils. Discover the Shadow that is attached to you by these fibers.

D: It feels like a mass of kelp. The fibers come from the kelp, enter my throat, and then go into my heart and my head.

M: With your eyes closed, notice the color of the kelp and the fibers.

D: Mostly dark, like blackness.

M: And when you touch them, what is the texture or temperature?

D: They're slimy.

M: And when you notice them attached to your throat, what is your emotional feeling?

D: Mostly fear. Also something like guilt. And some confusion.

M: You want to be congruent and speak your truth, but these dark, slimy, kelp-like fibers are preventing you, and you feel fear, guilt and some confusion. We know a lot about your Shadow now. In a moment, you can allow your hands to rest at your sides, and you can go inside and thank the parts of you that allowed you to discover the structure of your Shadow. (Dilts returns his hands to his sides.)

Finding the Positive Purpose of the Shadow Attachment

M: Now, imagine that your magical hands have become even more powerful. They have become laser empowered and can do anything. If you wanted to, for instance, you could just reach up with one or both of your hands and sever this connection to the Shadow. In a moment, I am going to ask you to lift your hands and seriously consider gouging out or severing the fibers. But don't actually do it; just get close to doing it. Seriously consider severing this attachment to the Shadow and notice how you feel emotionally as you are ready to do it. (Dilts slowly raises his hands, as if he were preparing to strike at the invisible fibers.)

What do you feel emotionally when you seriously consider severing this attachment and cutting off this Shadow forever?

D: I feel a combination of confusion and sadness.

M: You feel confusion and sadness. Now, bring your hands back down to your sides, because you're not going to cut this attachment. Your sense of confusion and sadness indicates that, internally, there's some positive function served by having the Shadow attached in this way. (Dilts lowers his hands.)

Some part of you allowed these dark, slimy fibers to come into your throat and down into your heart and up into your brain. Go inside and talk very gently to the part of you that allowed this enmeshment with these shadowy fibers. Ask that part of you, "Please tell me what is your positive purpose in having me be attached to this shadowy mass of kelp in this way"?

D: (Dilts stands in silence for a moment.) It is to protect me and somebody else. The positive purpose of this attachment is to protect me and somebody else from my own stupidity, ego and arrogance.

M: So, a part of you allowed this connection in order to protect you and someone else from your own stupidity, ego, arrogance. Say, "Thank you very much. This is very valuable. Any part of me that wants me to be protected is obviously a loyal part of me. And protecting others is also important to me. Thank you. "

D: (Dilts speaks quietly to himself.) Thank you.

M: And now please ask this protective part of you, "If you really succeeded in protecting me from my stupidity, ego, and arrogance, what would that do for me? What would I then get that is even more deeply important to me? What gift do you really want me to have?"

D: The answer I get is, "Truth."

M: To give you truth. That is extremely valuable. And you can say, "Thank you very much. I want the truth."

D: (Dilts speaks to himself.) Thank you very much. I want the truth.

M: And internally you might take a moment to discover what it would give you emotionally to have the truth. What is the emotional gift of 'truth'?

D: The feeling of wholeness . . . and love. I feel a sense of giving back love to that person I am trying to protect. She gave me a lot of life and a lot of love. There's so much that I got from her. Part of the positive purpose of allowing this attachment is to share some of it with her.

M: So, the emotional gift is to experience wholeness and share life and love, allowing what has come in to flow back out to others. It's like a feeling of gratitude.

D: Yes, gratitude.

M: So, this part of you has allowed the Shadow to come into you to try to make sure that you and somebody else are protected from your own ego, arrogance and stupidity in order to have truth, the experience of wholeness, and to gratefully share the love and life you have received from that other person. Please say to that part of you, "Thank you. I want this. It is a wonderful gift."

D: (Dilts speaks quietly to himself.) Thank you. I want this. It is awonderful gift.

Sculpting a "Spiritually Evolving" Self

M: Now, keeping in mind the positive purpose and gift of the part of you that has allowed the tendrils of the Shadow into your heart and brain, turn a little to your right. (Dilts turns slightly to his right.)

Using both of your magically empowered hands, begin to create a "spiritually evolving" Robert Dilts in front of you. This is not a regular Robert, it is a "spiritually evolving" Robert. He is able to be congruent and has the gifts of truth, love, wholeness and gratitude. He already has all of these wonderful qualities. (Dilts reaches his hands out in front of him, and begins moving them as if he is touching the outline of a body.)

As you sculpt this radiant Robert, realize that he does not have to be perfect. He looks just like you, is spiritually evolving and has a wonderful sense of humor. He keeps learning and changing and growing. Use your hands to create him, sculpting his entire body, all the way down to the floor. Sculpt his legs, knees, calf muscles and shin bones, all the way down to his feet on the floor. (Smiling, Dilts continues to move his hands as if sculpting a statue.)

Make sure that the "spiritually evolving" Robert Dilts is fully represented. Be sure that he is congruent and has the gifts of wholeness, truth, love and gratitude. It is not necessary to consciously know how he has been able to get these gifts. All you need to know is that he's the spiritually evolving you, and he's a step or two ahead of you in your spiritual evolution. Be sure to build his eyes, open and gleaming. (Dilts finishes sculpting and stands with his hands at his sides.)

Now, hold his face as though you were holding the face of a child, and blow the 'breath of life' into his nostrils, allowing him to be alive and radiant. (Dilts reaches out as if holding someone's face, blows gently, and then smiles broadly.)

This "spiritually evolving" Robert already has all of the resources and gifts that the protective part of you has been longing for. And his throat, heart and brain are completely free and clear. He would love to be able to connect with you. He would love to send his radiant, colorful fibers to you and be attached to you, but he can't, because you are currently occupied with these dark, slimy tendrils.

Notice how you feel about this wonderful Robert. Would you like to be connected to this spiritually evolving Robert Dilts and become more like him? (Dilts nods his head.)

Discovering the "Spiritually Evolving" Essence of the Shadow

M: Turn back to your left now and face the kelp. (Dilts turns slightly to the left.)

As you do, notice that an interesting thing has happened. On your right side you've created a "spiritually evolving" Robert. In front of you is the kelp. And, while you've been creating the spiritually evolving Robert, the "spiritually evolving essence" of the kelp has automatically appeared over to your left. This "spiritually evolving essence" of the kelp is exactly what the kelp really needs to be attached to. While you were creating the spiritually evolving Robert, this spiritually evolving essence of the kelp was created. The kelp that's attached to you really wants to be attached to its own spiritually evolving essence. Can you see the "spiritually evolving essence" of the kelp? What does it look like?

D: It's green and vibrant, like kelp in the ocean on a sunny day. In this form, it is the food for many forms of underwater life. I see this vibrant green kelp floating comfortably in a large aquarium.

Checking For Objections To Releasing The Shadow

M: Yes. This aquarium is the Shadow's proper place. And the "spiritually evolving" kelp in the aquarium would love to receive the dark, slimy kelp which is attached to your throat. But it can't because this shadowy kelp is attached to your throat. So it's up to you, with your magically empowered hands, to make a decision. First, you need to check whether you have any objection to releasing this Shadow from your throat. Go inside and ask the part of you that allowed the enmeshment connection with the Shadow kelp if it would object to releasing the fibers from your heart, throat and brain, attaching them to the spiritually evolving kelp in the aquarium, and then allowing the spiritually evolving Robert to attach to your throat, brain and heart. (Dilts stands quietly.)

If you experience any questions or objections, simply turn to the radiant spiritually evolving Robert on your right and ask him for his help and guidance. (Dilts turns to the right, and then back again.)

D: I don't sense any objection inside of me.

Releasing The Connection With The Shadow

M: Then, when you're ready, take all the time you need to very gently remove the kelp from your throat. Do it as if you were performing a sacred ceremony or ritual. Use your magical hands to reach up and tenderly remove all the fibers from your heart and your brain through your throat. (Dilts begins to move his hands as if gently pulling invisible threads from his throat.)

Be very gentle. There's no violence in this process. Tenderly and respectfully remove all of the attachments until every last remnant has left your body. Pull it all out through your throat, even the tiniest bit that might be lodged in your heart or in your brain. You can feel it coming out of your throat area. Every little bit. (Dilts continues the gentle pulling movements.)

Keep pulling until every last fiber has been removed. Your body will know when you are finished. (Dilts finishes the pulling movements and smiles.)

Attaching The Shadow To Its "Spiritually Evolving Essence"

M: Now gently take the fibers, and the Shadow kelp from which they come, and attach them to the "spiritually evolving essence" of the kelp in the aquarium. Do it such that the Shadow kelp is attached to the spiritually evolving kelp the way that it was attached to you. The shadow kelp becomes attached to spiritually evolving kelp by way of these fibers. Make sure that the Shadow kelp is all placed in its proper environment within the aquarium, where it will be loved, honored and respected. (Dilts moves his hands as if gathering up invisible threads and turns to his left. He makes motions as if threading many fibers together, then stands back, smiling.)

D: When I did that an interesting thing happened. It was as if the kelp had been covering up the spiritually evolving essence of the other person I was trying to protect. When I put the Shadow kelp in its proper place, I saw a shining image of the spiritual essence of the other person. She was smiling at me, and I knew she was together with her spiritual evolving self. It was very powerful.

Connecting With The "Spiritually Evolving" Self

M: And you can also notice that your own throat, brain and heart are free and available. And standing to your right is your own "spiritually evolving" self. This spiritually evolving Robert would love to be attached to your throat, heart and brain. With your magical hands you can find radiant, colorful fibers emanating from your spiritually evolving self. Some may come from his hands. Perhaps others come from his heart or brain. You can bring them out of his body and attach them to your body in exactly the same places that the Shadow's fibers were attached to you. You can bring these threads of light through your throat, into your brain, and down into the same place in your heart. (Dilts turns to the right and begins to make motions with his hands as if gathering threads from his spiritually evolving self and bringing them to his throat, heart and head.)

The spiritually evolving Robert is standing there, and these tendrils and fibers come from him into you, entering you in exactly the same way as the Shadow used to enter you.

D: There are different tendrils that come from different places, some from his fingers, some from his eyes, heart and throat.

M: And just continue to allow those fibers to come from him, into your throat, and spread throughout your body. Feel them filling you with congruence, truth, love, wholeness and gratitude. Notice that there is a message coming to you from the Spiritually Evolving Robert. As he comes closer to you, he whispers something in your ear. What does he say?

D: He's speaking to me softly saying, "You're loved."

Stabilizing The Transformation

M: Feel and hear the message, "You are loved," and let the Spiritually Evolving Robert fully attach to your body. As he does, you can welcome him home. You can say, "Welcome home Robert."

D: Welcome home Robert.

M: He's the one you've been thirsting for. He is your true spiritual companion now and forever who will never abandon you or hurt you. He will always be with you and continue to evolve. He's not static. He has a sense of humor and grows, evolves, and acquires new and more spiritual wholeness as he goes forward. The Spiritually Evolving Robert is with you, and the Shadow is now in its proper place where it can be provided for and honored.

Notice what kinds of internal changes occur as you think about your relationships with different people and imagine yourself in various times and places, now and tonight, and the next day and night, and the weeks and months and years from now. Think of special anniversaries, relationships, beginnings and endings, births and deaths. You will have your Spiritually Evolving Self with you, connected to you in this most intimate way. You can take your time and let me know what you're noticing, when you're ready.

D: A whole lot of things come up and are resolved. For example, I saw images of people who used to be connected with this Shadow, but now that the Shadow is in its proper place and I am connected with my spiritually evolving self, they are just people. There's no darkness or sadness, I just see them as individuals. All of my internal images seem to have more light in them. And a lot of things that have been associated with negative feelings or voices become transformed. They melt into a feeling of safety.

M: Wonderful. And you can just continue to allow that to evolve. Thank you, Robert.

D: Thank you very much. (Dilts and McDonald embrace. Applause.)

Releasing Enmeshment With The Shadow Graphic

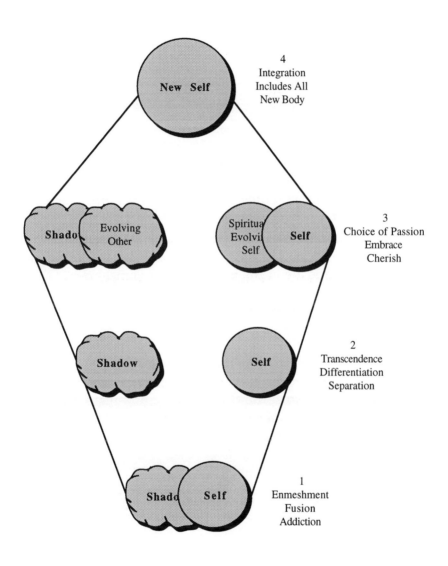

Summary of the Releasing Enmeshment With the Shadow Process
(The Archetype Patterns)

1. Touch your body where you feel a reaction or connection to the Shadow.

2. Now, while standing, <u>allow your hands to act on their own</u> and physically 'sculpt' a three dimensional representation of the Shadow wherever you feel its presence.

3. Once your hands have sculpted the Shadow, notice how you are attached, enmeshed or connected to it (for example, a cord connecting the two of you in some way; a heart-to-heart enmeshment; side-to-side; genitals to genitals; a beam of light; are you inside the Shadow?; is the Shadow inside of you?; etc.). Show with your hands and describe aloud the nature of this enmeshment, that is, what you see, hear and touch. (What is it? Where is it? What's it made of? How big is it? How does it feel to the touch? Etc.)

4. Imagine that you have "magical powers" in your hands. As you begin to use your magical hands to sever the enmeshment with the Shadow, <u>stop and just **consider** severing the connection</u>. Notice your emotional reaction to seriously considering the act of disconnecting.

5. Now, gently ask the part of you that has allowed this enmeshment to be established for its **positive purposes**. What are the actual benefits or gifts this connection is intended to provide in your life? Take your time here.

6. In a space a little to your right, sculpt your <u>Spiritually Evolving Self</u>: a holographic image of a You (your 'Big S' Self) who has <u>already</u> solved the issues and has the

resources necessary to be a <u>living example of the positive purposes</u> you just discovered in step 5. This You is wearing the clothes you're wearing and looks just like you. Yet this <u>Spiritually Evolving Self</u> is just steps ahead of you, loves you, has a sense of humor, and will always be with you, now and in the future. Blow the breath of life into the nostrils of your <u>Spiritually Evolving Self</u>. Now inhale the breath of new life coming from this deeper You.

7. Notice that while you were 'sculpting' your own <u>Spiritually Evolving Self</u>, a holographic representation of the 'spiritual essence' of the Shadow has appeared to your left. This 'spiritual essence' of the Shadow wants to be connected to the Shadow. So, gently ask yourself if there is any part of you that objects to disconnecting the Shadow from your body, connecting it to its 'spiritual essence', and then connecting yourself to your <u>Spiritual Evolving Self</u>. If there is any objection, simply turn to your right, face your <u>Spiritually Evolving Self</u> and ask if he or she is fully ready to receive you and handle the objection.

8. When you're ready, gently release your enmeshment with the Shadow (sever it, melt it, move it, or whatever). And help the Shadow connect to its 'spiritual essence' <u>in **precisely** the same way</u> that it had been connected with you.

9. Now, turn and <u>connect with your Spiritually Evolving Self in **precisely** the same way</u> that you were connected to the Shadow. Here are some examples: If the Shadow is like a sword in your throat, then your <u>Spiritually Evolving Self</u> should initially take the form of a sword which you place in your throat, then allow this type of connection to change to its most appropriate form. If you are inside the Shadow, then your goal

is to end up inside the <u>Spiritually Evolving Self</u>. If you are connected to the Shadow by a cord, then your goal is to connect to your <u>Spiritually Evolving Self</u> by the cord. In any case, you are finished when you have <u>precisely the same enmeshment form, but new content</u>.

10. Now, **see** your <u>Spiritually Evolving Self</u>, **feel** your bodily connections and **listen** as he or she welcomes you home and whispers something personal in your ear.

11. Notice your here-and-now experience with your <u>Spiritually Evolving Self</u>: being in this moment, in this place, with these people, and these possibilities, etc.

Discussion of the Releasing Enmeshment Process

M: The Releasing Enmeshment procedure is a very kines-thetic, bodily oriented process. The physical emphasis on sculpting the structure of the enmeshment is to help you come more and more into your body. You actually feel the Shadow attachment as you sculpt it.

D: You want to feel exactly how you are connected.

M: That's why I asked Robert, "How does it feel? Where is it? How deep does it go?" I wanted his body to be engaged.

The Releasing Enmeshment with the Shadow process is derived from a format for Releasing Emotional Enmesh-ment that I developed in 1988 in order to help people resolve co-dependence. In the 1980's I was exploring the structure of addiction in the form of co-dependence. I wanted to uncover the structure of co-dependence in order to transform it. I discovered that people who experienced themselves as co-dependent often had these types of concrete representations of enmeshment. I found that people who were alcoholic or addicted often experienced an "enmeshment" with another person. It was as though they didn't know where they ended and a certain other person began. They felt as if they were "Siamese twins" with this other person.

As I was developing it, Connirae Andreas reminded me to look for the positive purpose of the enmeshment. And when we assume a positive purpose it is easier to do non-violent change work. In the end, the resolution of co-dependence or any addiction does not occur in an atmosphere of violence. If the Shadow is violently and disrespectfully cut off, it comes back again, because it is dishonored and it has no place to go. A major reason this process works and keeps working is because there's no violence. We do not simply cut off the connection. We do not attack the enmeshed Shadow. We gently remove the connection and respectfully give the Shadow a place of honor. This is the secret of how true change happens. Love that which you have regarded as your enemy. Find a way to genuinely include it.

Releasing Enmeshment with the Shadow involves love and kindness in relationship to what we have previously called the "Shadow." One purpose of the process is to allow the Shadow to have its place, where it can be respected and honored.

In doing this process it is important that you notice how the Shadow is represented. Then your hands become magically empowered, so you can create a Spiritually Evolving Self. But you don't create the Spiritually Evolving Self until you discover the positive purpose of the part of you that allowed the enmeshment into your life and body. In my view, our whole lives are based on positive purpose. All our unconscious mind wants to do is take care of us.

Contrary to popular belief, I think the unconscious mind functions through love. When you find your enmeshment, ask yourself, "What was the positive purpose of getting enmeshed with this Shadow in the first place?" Then build a Spiritually Evolving Self who already has those positive qualities. Then, in a very gentle way, you remove the Shadow and prepare to have it connect with its spiritually evolving essence. If you have no objection, attach yourself to your Spiritually Evolving Self, in precisely the same way that you had been attached to the Shadow. Even though it might seem weird to become enmeshed with your Spiritually Evolving Self, you do so in order to match the attachment you used to have with the Shadow. In the end, you want to have the same form with different content. Your whole system will recognize the form and thus accept the new content.

D: That was an important point for me just now in my work with my Shadow. I initially thought, "I don't want tendrils coming in my throat at all." It was the tendrils coming in my throat that seemed to be the bad thing. And yet there was a lot of message value for me to have my evolving self coming in through my throat. It was really changed. And then the form also changed, it didn't remain tendrils. It kept evolving into a kind of an energy, a kind of light.

When I was sculpting the spiritually evolving Robert, it was important that I took my time. I needed to spend time with his throat, heart and head. One of the things that came to me while I was sculpting him was how much the throat was a focal point between the head and the heart. I think the reason the enmeshment was in the throat was because that's the connection-point between the head and the heart. So it was important for me to take my time there.

When I put the shadowy tendrils into the spiritually evolving kelp, their color changed. Instead of being dark, slimy threads, they became flat and green like plants. They became alive and had many sparkling colors.

When I placed the threads from my spiritually evolving self into my throat, I felt my hands and body tingling. The tendrils transformed into threads of sparkling, colored light.

Handling Possible Objections

D: As Robert McDonald demonstrated with me, a good way to handle most objections to releasing your Shadow is to utilize the Spiritually Evolving Self. If you discover an objection, turn and ask your Spiritually Evolving Self, "How will this objection be handled?" Almost always you'll get the answer or the insight. Remember, you've built into the Spiritually Evolving Self all the resources that are needed.

M: If a part of you comes up with an objection simply ask, "What is your objection, specifically?" Then ask the Spiritually Evolving Self for a way to handle the objection, knowing that he or she already has all the resources needed to handle it.

Also, 'meta-outcomes' are very important to this process. A meta-outcome is 'the outcome of an outcome'. For example, if my outcome is to have a new car, you would elicit my 'meta outcome' by asking, "What would having a new car do for you?" I might answer, "If I had a new car I would feel powerful." In that case, feeling powerful is my first meta-outcome. You could continue by asking, "If you get to feel powerful, what's that going to give you?" I might say something like, "Then I'll have self-esteem." Self esteem is the 'meta outcome' of feeling powerful. You could go even deeper by asking, "If you had self-esteem, what would that give you?" I might answer, "Joy."

In doing Releasing Enmeshment With The Shadow it is important to reach a meta outcome that is emotionally based and unobjectionable. For instance, no one objects to joy. Somebody might object to a new car, but nobody objects to joy.

D: For example, when Robert initially asked for the positive purpose or 'meta outcome' of my enmeshment with the dark, slimy fibers, I responded that it was to protect myself and somebody else from my own ego, arrogance and stupidity. Robert guided me to find an even deeper level meta outcome, which was to have truth. Finally, we discovered that the emotional and unobjectionable meta outcome of truth was the experience of wholeness, gratitude and sharing love and life.

When you have been able to identify the positive purposes and high level meta outcomes of the enmeshment, then it is easy to remove the Shadow and place it in it's proper place. You don't have to yank or pull it out. It flows out easily. And when you have released the Shadow, there's no telling what kind of impact it might have.

For a woman in one of our programs, the Shadow was an inability to forgive that she represented as a mace - a medieval weapon made of an iron ball with a bunch of spikes sticking out of it. As a result of the Releasing Enmeshment with the Shadow process, she let go of this mace and placed it into her museum of personal history. When she was finished, she began thinking about a former friend of hers whom she had not seen in over 12 years because of a disagreement. After 12 years she was finally able forgive this person. When she got home that night, there was a message on her telephone answering machine from this particular friend. The message said, "I decided to track you down after all these years. I have been thinking of you and felt the need to speak to you."

Releasing Enmeshment as a Path to Spiritual Growth

M: Releasing Enmeshment With The Shadow is an ongoing process of personal and spiritual growth. As many times as Robert and I have done this, we always find a new Shadow.

D: As we said earlier, wherever there's Light, there's a Shadow. What happens for me is when one Shadow is gone and I grow, more light emerges. As long as there's more Light, there will be more Shadow.

M: In my opinion, our ultimate spiritual work is to love life and death, Light and Shadow. Perhaps loving duality is the road to the non-dual. In the Releasing Enmeshment With The Shadow process we are opening to loving that which we previously feared. We learn to respect and honor it. Each time we do that, a greater amount of Light comes to us and through us. We grow. We include more.

D: Therefore, finding another Shadow doesn't mean I'm broken. Rather, my task is to find and release my Shadows. When I do, there is a brilliant burst of Light, and then I go on. I naturally evolve. It's like shining a light on a plant that's been in the dark.

Darkness doesn't shine into light. Darkness is simply the absence of light. Light shines into darkness but it doesn't go the other way around. So the Shadow shows me a place where the Light isn't shining in. And this process is a way to get the Light into that place where it needs to be.

M: We continue on the path to greater and greater Light, greater and greater love.

Robert McDonald's Shadow Work

M: Every time Robert and I teach <u>Tools of the Spirit</u>, we demonstrate the Releasing Enmeshment With The Shadow process by going through it ourselves. There is no end to the work of transcending and including the Shadow. One instance of doing my own Shadow work stands out to me. The Shadow I found was particularly disturbing, and therefore particularly fruitful. When I opened myself to the Shadow, I immediately got an intense reaction in my groin. It felt as though my testicles were being grabbed. As I allowed my "magically empowered hands" to sculpt whatever was causing the pain, I discovered a hand on my testicles. The hand belonged to an arm which somehow emerged from the ground. Soon I discovered an old man, perhaps an Eskimo, probably an oriental priest, dressed in a hooded robe. The old man was lying on his back underground, and he had reached his hand up from the ground to grab me by the testicles. I couldn't move. With further exploration, I discovered that he, himself was attached to an endless number of other oriental priests, going back in time for endless generations.

When Robert asked me how I felt about severing the connection to the oriental priest, I felt a deep sense of loss and wept. I learned that the positive purpose of the part of me that allowed the Shadow to attach to me in this way was to provide me with stability and keep me on the ground. So, I allowed my "magically empowered hands" to create a Spiritually Evolving Robert who already had stability and could easily remain on the ground. After I removed the oriental priest's hand from my testicles and attached him to the Spiritually Evolving Shadow (an evolving oriental priest), the Spiritually Evolving Robert easily laid down underground and gently held my testicles. As he did this, an infinite number of Spiritually Evolving Roberts appeared. All of them connected to the one who attached himself to me.

In an instant, the Spiritually Evolving Robert let go of my testicles and placed his index finger at the base of my tail bone. I felt an intense rush of energy, moving quickly up my spine. And when I looked, as far as I could see, there were generations upon generations of Spiritually Evolving Roberts, lying underground, holding hands with each other. In that moment I noticed that together they created a river of golden Light. It flowed from all the generations that preceded me, from the unremembered past, into my spine and connected me to a great tradition of Love and Compassion, forever.

The Emperor's Looking-Glass

D: There is an old tale about the Emperor of China which I think illustrates the value of finding the shadow and putting it in its proper place. It seems that he had a magical looking-glass. Whoever gazed upon the mirror saw not his or her own image, but only that of the Emperor. One day one of the Emperor's oldest and most loyal courtiers humbly asked if he might have the mirror so that he could always be near the Emperor's exalted image. Although he was hesitant to part with his prized treasure, the Emperor was flattered by the courtier's request and allowed him the supreme honor of taking the mirror to his home.

Sometime later the Emperor dropped by the residence of the courtier unannounced. He was surprised to find that, rather having a prominent place, his precious mirror was sitting, covered with dust, in a dingy sideroom. Feeling that he had been made a fool of by the ungrateful courtier, the Emperor slammed his fist in anger, accidentally shattering the mirror and severely cutting his hand. In his rage the Emperor ordered the immediate arrest of the courtier, and had him flogged and thrown into prison.

The Emperor then had his special looking-glass carefully repaired and returned to him. To his amazement, when he looked in the mirror he saw the image of an ass with a bloody bandage on its front hoof. He suddenly realized that this was the image everyone else had always seen but had feared to report. The faithful courtier had asked for the mirror in order to save the Emperor from further ridicule.

Humbled, the Emperor had the courtier released from prison and restored to his position at the palace. He begged the courtier's forgiveness and made him his top advisor. The Emperor then ordered the mirror to be set into the back of his throne, so he would never forget the lesson he had learned about his own arrogance, blindness and temper.

After that, the Emperor reigned for many years with wisdom, compassion and humility. One day the Emperor quietly died in his sleep while on the throne. At the moment of his passing, the whole court saw the image of the ass in the mirror transform into the luminous form of an angel, which remains to this day.

Saying Goodbye

D: Albert Einstein said it is a wonderful thing that there's a natural limit to a human life, because, when it's over we can look back on it as a completed work of art. If it didn't end we couldn't see it as a whole. Saying goodbye is an acknowledgment that something is over and can be looked upon as complete.

Consider the end of the last day of a workshop when people are saying goodbye. It's oftentimes very emotional. People say special things to those who touched them in some way, expressing gratitude.

M: Perhaps they exchange cards and promise to call each other. Maybe they finally get around to asking specific questions about where they live and tell each other how good it was to be together.

D: They might say one another, "I really appreciate you. You were really great."

M: In other words, the whole time during the workshop they might have been thinking, "That person really is a lot like me and I'd like to tell him or her, 'I like you'. But I'll wait til the last day." And then on the last day they go to the person and say, "I wish I had more time to tell you how I feel but, we only have a minute because I've got to get to the airport."

D: They have begun to open up to something deeper, and then they have to leave, and probably won't see each other again.

M: Think of how many times you've had an experience like that.

In the days when I was doing a lot of therapy, I noticed that often in the last 5 minutes a client would tell me what he or she really came for. They would tell me when they were just about ready to leave. I've noticed that in the last few minutes of some workshops, people seem more likely to tell deeper truths to each other . . . just before they leave. They say things like, "I'm really glad that you were here; you touched me with what you were saying and who you were, and I'd like a hug. I hope to see you again." Have you ever done that?

D: When we were planning *Tools of the Spirit* Robert and I thought, "What would happen if we said goodbye in the middle of the workshop, instead of at the end?" We decided to pretend that the workshop was over, and say goodbye.

M: We tell a closing metaphor. Then we put on our shoes and socks and jackets, and act as if we are all leaving.

D: In this way, people have the opportunity to say the things to one another that they usually save until the end.

M: It's almost like the opposite of family secrets. Family secrets are those secrets that are kept away from others because we want to protect the family from pain. But the secrets we shyly reveal at the end of workshops, or at the end of powerfully emotionally connective experiences, are kept during the workshop because we are not ready to tell others how good we feel. We want to wait, to save it. By saying "goodbye" in the middle of the workshop we have a chance to tell others how we really feel.

D: Oftentimes when something is over and I look back on it, I ask myself what I am grateful for. While the experience is happening I tend to notice what is missing. At the end of a seminar, I'll notice how grateful I am for the things that did happen. For instance, I might recognize how grateful I am for the opportunity to fulfill a dream. I can remember when *Tools of the Spirit* was just a dream that Robert and I had. We had a dream that one day we'd be sharing our deepest and most intimate spiritual experiences with many other people. Now it's not a dream anymore, it's reality.

Sometimes I forget that this used to be only a dream. Now that it's happened, it's just another "lousy day in paradise." When I remember that it used to be a dream, I feel a lot of gratitude. I wouldn't have the opportunity to feel that gratitude if *Tools of the Spirit* didn't end.

The Monk And The Tiger

M: I believe most deeply that what's asked of me is to love all of God's creation, and that means everything, including what I haven't regarded as worthy of love. I believe that is what's asked of me and everyone on Earth. Which reminds me of the story of a monk who was running in the forest. He was running and running because there was a gigantic tiger chasing him. The monk was in mortal danger. So he ran as fast as he could. He was out of breath and he was sweating, and struggling, and frightened and his heart was beating very fast. He thought he could escape if he could just make it over the ridge in the distance.

When he got over the ridge, however, he almost fell off a cliff. As he stood at the cliff the tiger was coming closer and closer. He looked down and thought, "It's too far to jump to the bottom." So nearing panic, he looked over the cliff and noticed a little branch, growing out of it, a few feet down. Perhaps it would hold his weight and he could hang on to it. So he slipped over the edge of the cliff, just as the tiger reached him. As he lowered himself over the cliff, he could feel the breath of the tiger above him.

And just at that time, the monk looked down and saw something even more frightening. Below him, at the bottom of the cliff, patiently waiting, was another tiger. Almost in despair, the monk held even more tightly to the branch. Soon he was very tired. And as he gripped the branch, feeling frightened, he looked up and saw the tiger above him, growling. And he looked down at the tiger below him, growling. And to make matters even worse, he felt the branch start to slowly give way. His heart was racing. He was terrified.

But just then, the monk looked over to his right and he saw a little leaf growing out of the side of the cliff. And near the leaf was a beautiful strawberry. He looked at the strawberry and he tried to hold on. He looked up at the tiger above him, and he looked down at the tiger below him, and he looked at the strawberry. And just before the branch gave way, the monk took a breath, reached over and picked the strawberry. He brought it close to his face and smelled it. And when he bit into the strawberry, it was the most delicious thing he had ever tasted.

Chapter 8

Self Parenting

Overview of Chapter 8

- **My Friend John and the Tiger**
- **Forgive and Remember**
- **The Self-Parenting Process**
- **Summary of the Self-Parenting Process**

'My Friend John' and the Tiger

M: I would like to tell you a story about my friend John. John lived most of his life indoors, in a big inner city. The only animals he'd ever seen were a few stray cats, dogs and an occasional rat. So, when he got old enough to wonder what the rest of the world was like, he simply went for a walk and began to explore his neighborhood. After a few miles, he walked by the city zoo. He'd never been to the Zoo before, but he could hear some of the animal sounds and he became so curious he bought a ticket and walked in. John was truly amazed! He saw the long necked giraffes, the huge gorillas, and even a rhino. He'd never seen these animals before. But when he walked up to a tiger's cage, he said, "Oh, I know you. You're a cat. A very large cat. And I love cats." He put his hand into the tiger's cage to pet the cat. The tiger mauled his hand. John screamed. His hand was bleeding. He had to be taken to the local hospital where the wound was cleaned and sewn up; then his hand was bandaged and rendered immobile. It took him weeks to recover. And all during his recovery time, whenever he would think of that big cat he would get angry. He couldn't stand even the thought of the big cat.

But one day he missed the Zoo so much that he returned to visit it again. He was very happy when he saw the giraffes, gorillas and rhinos; he loved them. But he couldn't get near the tiger's cage without feeling terrible inside. Just knowing where the tiger lived in the Zoo upset him. He thought he'd get over it but he didn't.

After a long while, he asked someone on the street how he could feel comfortable around the tiger. The stranger said, "Well, everybody knows that when you are hurt, you must learn to forgive and forget." John thought this was a marvelous idea. He decided right then and there to forgive and forget. And the next day he happily walked into the Zoo and saw the giraffes, the gorillas and the rhinos, and he loved them. When he walked up to the tiger's cage, he felt very good. He said, "Cat, I have completely forgiven and forgotten everything. And I feel wonderful!" In his joy he reached his hand into the cage to pet the big cat. The tiger mauled his hand, again. John screamed. His hand was bleeding. He had to be taken to the local hospital where the wound was cleaned and sewn up; his hand was bandaged and rendered immobile. It took him weeks to recover.

Well, this time he was so upset by what the big cat had done to him that he had to see a therapist. I think he actually saw an NLP practitioner. After he explained his dilemma to the practitioner, she said, "Well, forgiveness will help you a lot." John said, "Oh, no you don't. I've tried that and it doesn't work." The therapist responded, "I mean perhaps you could try forgiving and remembering. Forgive in order to let go of your hurt, and *remember* in order to accept the way things are."

The next day John walked into the Zoo and saw the giraffes, gorillas and the rhinos, and he loved them. And when he walked up to the tiger's cage, he kept a respectful distance, and said, "I forgive you. I see now that you are not simply a big cat. I thought you were something you are not. I am sorry. You are a tiger and you do what tigers can be expected to do. And I will remember. See you next time."

Forgive and Remember

M: How do we go about forgiving the unforgivable? Many people have said they couldn't possibly forgive certain acts, certain ways they were treated. Indeed, it is possible to regard forgiveness as an irrational act. From this perspective, the most rational thing to do when hurt by someone else is to either hurt that person in return or hold a grudge, nursing the deep feelings of hurt. In other words, the rational person, when hurt, will protect him or herself for as long as it takes to ensure survival. From a rational point of view, to risk survival seems foolish and unacceptable, particularly if we were devastated by the very people who were supposed to protect us - our parents, for example.

As they say in _The Course In Miracles_, I believe there are two categories of emotions: fear and love. That is, all negative emotions base their existence on fear (the anticipation of meaningless pain). Therefore, if there were no fear there would be no hurt, anger, rage, depression, grief, need for revenge, etc. And love can be thought of as the opposite of fear. Interestingly, most of us seem to think we should get rid of our fear, destroy it, or remove it in some way and simply keep love as the remainder. But I've noticed that when love and fear are regarded as opposites, I cannot have one without the other; they arise simultaneously. They define each other in a duality.

In my view, there is a "transcendent Love," and with this Love we can learn to 'Love our fear' and 'Love our love'. This notion might seem irrational or impossible. But, on the rational level, we could define this transcendent Love as "forgiveness". I call it "transcendent Love" because it transcends the apparent conflict between our usual understanding of fear and love. Transcendent Love is at a higher level and includes both fear and love. It is beyond fear and love but it embraces them both. And, to me the bridge from fear to love is forgiveness.

Some people have had such powerfully negative experiences that they say, "I couldn't possibly forgive." Some people advise them to forgive and forget. And sometimes that works out. Another way would be to forgive and remember. It's like placing the Shadow in its proper place. For instance, if you place reminders of the Holocaust in a museum, you won't forget the horror, you will remember what happened. But remembering does not have to be a refusal to forgive.

D: Similarly, 'to forgive' does not have to mean 'to forget'. If we say, "Never forget, never forgive, never again," the implication is that in order to remember a violation and prevent it from happening again, you must never forgive. From our perspective the challenge is to forgive and learn.

M: How is it possible to forgive and learn, even from the most horrible crimes? Just as you did when you were working with your Shadow, it is necessary to understand that behind every behavior is a positive intention. Some people might wonder, "How could we possibly do that and remain human?" On the other hand, how can we presume negative purposes and remain human?

Maybe our humanity has something to do with the ability to go beyond any limitation that we've ever thought of. A completely rational person does not forgive anything or anybody, because rationality wants to make sure the body survives. So forgiveness can be perceived as an irrational act. But forgiving is ultimately a spiritual act. At the bottom of being deeply human, past all the crust and the hurt and the scars, is something that continually finds a fountain of innocence. I'm convinced that each and every one of us is innocent, absolutely innocent. No matter what the behavior is, the being is innocent. Being and behavior are different levels. No matter what I've done, in my essence I'm innocent. Everyone is. The question is, "How do we bring this awareness into our bodies?"

D: The Self Parenting Process is a format developed by Robert McDonald to help answer this important question. It is a process by which you are able to forgive and remember by applying the principle of positive intention to discover the fundamental innocence of yourself and others.

M: Most people I meet have some unfinished business with their mother and father; something that needs to be forgiven. It may be some kind of unresolved pain, hurt or feelings of abandonment. On the other hand, unfinished business with Mother and Father may be positive; it may simply be an unexpressed need to praise, love and celebrate. But unfinished business, whether positive or negative in nature, simply awaits completion.

"Imprinting" and the Self Parenting Process

D: In considering our relationships with 'mother' and 'father' it is important to realize that there's a biological mother and father, and there's what could be called the "archetypic" mother and father. An illustration of an "archetypic" parent is the phenomenon of "imprinting," which can be easily observed in the behavior of newly hatched ducklings. When a duckling is first born, it instinctively knows that it needs to find a "mother" in order to survive. But the duckling is not born with a picture of its mother in its mind. It doesn't know that she's got a yellow beak, white feathers and webbed feet. It knows "mother" at the level of deep structure, but does not know the details of her surface structure. The only thing it knows biologically is that its mother moves. And it knows it has to find her.

Thus, the duckling is born with internal archetypes of key relationships, such as "mother," already in place. It does not need to learn that it needs a mother, it is born *knowing* that it needs a mother, and that it should follow her and learn how to act in the world from her. What the duckling needs to learn is what its "mother" looks like. If its biological mother isn't around after its birth for some reason, the duckling will follow whatever moves. And the duckling eventually forms what's called an "imprint" of the animal or object it is following. That imprint is its representation of its "mother." After a certain period of time, even if you bring back the real mother, the duckling will ignore its biological mother and follow the imprinted mother.

Something parallel to this is present in human beings. "Mother" and "Father" are very deep archetypic relationships that come from many millions of years of evolution.

M: One way to access a model of an archetypic mother or father is to think of the father or the mother that you have or had. Of course some people may not have ever known their biological parents. In this case they simply need to notice the many "mothers" and "fathers" they've had in their lives. There is a deeper space that your biological or sociological parents filled. There's an archetypic structure that those human beings filled.

D: The people who were your biological parents may or may not be your spiritual parents. Robert McDonald's Self Parenting process can be used with either biological or 'archetypic' parents.

The Self Parenting Process

M: To begin this process it is important to be seated in a way that's comfortable for you. Make sure your back, legs and feet are comfortable. If you have any tension in your body, simply breathe there. Sit with your hands palm-up on your upper thighs. Put your hands several inches apart, so that they are not touching each other.

D: Allow yourself to enter a state of contemplation, meditation and openness to whatever messages and communications are most important for you.

M: Breathe into your body. Allow the air to come in, filling your lungs and spreading down into your body. When you exhale, let a small sigh come from your mouth, almost like saying, "Ahhhh." How does it feel to hear and sense your own sigh? Notice how it can help to deepen your sense of relaxation.

Finding the Symbol of the Mother

D: As you become even more in touch with yourself at many different levels, begin to think about your mother, or <u>The</u> Mother. Notice the feelings that you have associated with your mother or The Mother. Allow those feelings to begin to intensify and notice <u>where in your body you feel the sense of your mother</u>? Where does your 'mother' live in your body? Where do you feel her presence? When you have the sense of where your mother or The Mother lives in your body, take your <u>left</u> hand and touch that part of your body.

Intensify the feeling of your mother beneath your left hand more and more. Then return your hand to your lap, placing it palm-up. As you do that, allow the feeling associated with your mother to dislodge from its location in your body and begin to move to your left shoulder, down your left arm and into your left hand. Let the feeling of your mother begin to free itself from where it has been in your body and flow into your left hand. Feel every molecule, every bit of your mother dislodging from the place where she's been living in your body and move, journey and migrate through your left shoulder, down your left arm and into the open palm of your left hand. As it collects there, notice that it begins to take shape and become an image or symbol that you can see. If you could see it, what image does your mother take? Perhaps you see a flower, or an angel. Perhaps you see a stone, a ship, or a tower.

Whatever symbol you see, welcome your mother's image in your left hand. Say to the image, in your birth language, "Welcome mother. I asked you to come and you came. Thank you for coming and revealing yourself to me." Even if it seems strange at first, say this very ceremonially and respectfully in your own way. Say to that image in your hand. "Thank you mother. I asked you to come and you came." And notice that she's there.

Then in a very gentle voice, and with great respect, please say to this image, "Mother, I'm going to turn my attention elsewhere for awhile. Please excuse me. I will come back."

Finding the Symbol of the Father

M: Then, gently and respectfully move your attention away from your left hand, leaving your mother there, knowing that you can once again go deeply inside of yourself. Notice what happens when you begin to think about your father or The Father. What feelings do you have when you think about your father or The Father. When you think about your 'father', where in your body do you feel him living? Where is the place that your father resides? When you're ready, use your right hand to touch the part of your body where you feel your father residing. Touch that part very gently and leave your hand there for awhile.

Intensify the feeling of your father in your body. Then, let your right hand return to its place palm-up on your leg. Allow the feeling of your father to dislodge from its location and begin to move, travel, migrate and journey over to your right shoulder and down your right arm, like a stream or river which pools in your right hand. Feel your father going down your right arm, through your right bicep, down your right forearm, across your right wrist, and into your right hand. Feel every bit of your father, even the last tiny molecule that has been in your body, leave that part of your body, move down your right arm, and pool in your right hand. And as it pools it begins to take shape. I wonder what form he will take? I wonder what you'll see, what symbol will represent your father? If the feeling in your right hand were to become an image or symbol that you could see, what would it be? If you don't have an image of your father in your right hand, just imagine that you did. What symbol would it be?

Perhaps you see an ocean storm, coal, a lighthouse or a boulder of granite. Whatever image you see, say, "Thank you for coming father. I asked you to come. Even if we have been at odds or there has been great distance between us, I asked you to come and you're here. Thank you for coming, father."

Then, say to the image of your father in your right hand, "Excuse me father, I'm going to turn my attention elsewhere. I'll be back." Then very gently turn your head away from communicating with your father.

Finding the Gift of the Mother

D: Then begin to turn your head back to your left hand and notice that the image of your mother is still in your left hand. Say to her, very respectfully, "Mother, I said I'd be back and I'm back. Thank you for waiting." Acknowledge her for waiting while you've been talking to your father. Then say, "Mother, I have an important question that I'd like to ask you. The question is, 'What is your positive purpose? What is the gift that you've been trying to give me all of my life?'" Even if you've had a very difficult time with your biological mother, even if there's been conflict or distance, you respectfully ask, "What is the gift that you've wanted to give me all of my life?" And listen. If she says something negative like, "I've been trying to hurt you or punish you," say, "I understand mother, but please tell me, what is the positive gift that you've been trying to give me by punishing me? What is it that you've really wanted for me?"

It's important to know that this is a genuine gift that you accept, no strings attached. If you don't like the gift, if it's one of harm, you simply ask, "What is the gift you're trying to give me by harming me?" Find the gift by very gently asking that question. And when you know the gift, and you're willing to accept it, no strings attached, then say, "I accept your gift mother, no strings attached."

If the gift is something like "love" or "understanding," you can say, "I accept the gift mother, thank you."

And when you've been able to identify your mother's positive purpose, the true gift that she's been trying to give you all of your life, and you've accepted it, please say to her, "Thank you mother. I'm going to turn my attention elsewhere again for a moment. But I will be back. Excuse me."

Finding the Gift of the Father

M: Turning your head slowly, shift your attention gently over
to your father in your right hand and say, "Father, I have
come back. I told you I would return. Thank you for
waiting." Then ask your father, "Father, please tell me
what is the gift you have been trying to give me all of my
life?" And listen for his answer.

Even if you think that what you received from your
biological father was not a gift, or that he didn't want to
give you anything, just ask him, "What is the gift you
were trying to give me, that you would have loved to give
me if you could have?"

If your father says his gift was something like "detachment," and you don't want that, then you ask, "Father,
what is it that you wanted me to have by giving me
detachment?" He might answer that he didn't want you to
be hurt, that he wanted you to be safe and protected from
pain. And this might be a gift that you want and can
accept.

If he says, "I was trying to make life easy for you," say,
"Thank you father." And you could even go beyond that.
You could say to him, "Well father, if you could have made
life easy for me, what gift would I have received by having
an easier life? What would 'having an easier life' give me
that you really would like me to have?" Notice what he
tells you. Perhaps he responds, "Fun." And you can say,
"Thank you father, I want fun. It's so wonderful. I can
accept fun, no strings attached."

Your father might answer, "Strength and an instinct to
survive." If you want that, you can say, "Thank you
father. I accept this gift, no strings attached."

When you've found the gift that you can accept, no
strings attached, say to your father, "Thank you father.
I'm going to turn my attention elsewhere again for a
moment. But I will be back. Please excuse me."

Helping the Mother Understand the Gift of the Father

D: Allow yourself to turn your attention to your mother in your left. Greet your mother and say very politely and kindly, "Hello mother, thank you for waiting. I said that I would be back and I'm back." And then say, "Mother, I have a very important question for you. You have heard what father's gift has been for me. And even though you and father have not necessarily gotten along, maybe you even fought, disliked one another or even hated each other at some points, but mother, I'd like to ask if you can understand and appreciate the value of father's gift to me?"

You are not asking your mother to understand or accept your father's behavior. You want her to appreciate that your father's gift, this beautiful, wonderful gift, is important to you. You are only asking her to understand and appreciate the value of the gift to you. So, if your father's gift was "fun," you would ask your mother, "Can you understand and appreciate the value of the gift of fun for me?" If the father's gift was "strength and the instinct to survive," you would ask your mother, "Mother, can you understand and appreciate the value to me of the gift of 'strength and the instinct to survive'?"

Your mother doesn't have to accept your father, and she doesn't have to accept the way that your father tried to give his gift to you. She only needs to understand and appreciate the value of his gift for you. And if she's not able to understand its value to you, just gently and respectfully explain it to her, saying, "Mother, this is why that gift is valuable for me."

When your mother is able to understand and appreciate the value of your father's gift for you, say, "Thank you for your understanding mother. Now please excuse me. One more time I'm going to turn my attention elsewhere for a moment, but I will be back."

Helping the Father Understand the Gift of the Mother

M: As you excuse yourself from your mother, bring your attention over to your right hand where your father is. And say, "Father, I told you I'd come back and I'm back. I'd like to ask you a very important question. Can you understand and appreciate the value of the gift that my mother has for me? Can you understand and appreciate how important this gift is for me; not her behavior, but the gift she's been trying to give me?" And notice your father's response.

And once again your father does not have to accept the behavior of your mother. He does not have to accept the way in which she attempted to give you her gift. It's only important for your father to understand and appreciate the value of your mother's gift for you.

And when your father lets you know that he can understand and appreciate the value of your mother's gift for you, gently say, "Thank you father. I'm glad that you can understand and appreciate mother's gift, because her gift is so important to me."

Integrating the Mother and the Father

M: Very gently bring your attention now to the area between your father and mother, so that you notice them both, your mother in your left hand and your father in your right hand. And say to them, "For the first time, the two of you recognize and appreciate each other's gifts for me. I know that you have been at odds within me at times. I know there have been difficulties. And yet for the first time you understand and appreciate each other's gifts for me. I thank you for this."

D: And you can explain to them in your own words the need for them to work together in new and more effective ways in order for you to receive the gifts that they each have for you.

M: You can say to them, "What you've done in the past, separately, hasn't worked. I need something new. I need you to come together in a way that creates something new, a new possibility, a new way of being."

D: And then lift your hands very gently a little bit above your lap and turn your hands so that the left palm faces the right palm.

M: Both palms face each other a little above your lap. Don't worry, your parents won't fall out. Allow your palms to face each other as though your hands are going to clap. As you slowly and gently face them towards one another, begin to feel the two energies between your hands.

D: Allow your hands to begin to move towards one another.

M: Slowly, very slowly, an integration is beginning. Both of these images are longing to create something new for you. Watch and feel as the images of mother and father begin to merge and mingle, and mix and integrate.

D: Feel both of them gently coming together and integrating as your hands get closer and closer.

M: Your fingers touch, and your hands begin pressing together. Mother and father are swirling between your hands, mixing, mingling and merging.

D: As your hands join, press them together, letting them do their work.

M: When your hands are ready to open, they will gently make a little space, like a lotus flower opening. I wonder what you'll find, what image you'll notice. What's there?

D: Open your hands now to discover the new image that represents the full integration and synthesis of mother and father.

M: What was separate is now one.

D: What do you see?

M: If you could see it now, what is this symbol?

D: For instance, if your mother's symbol were a bird and the father's symbol were a light house, they might combine to create a guardian angel. A flower and a stone might become a crystal. A tower and an ocean storm might become a waterfall. You can allow your unconscious mind to create your own synthesis of the symbols of your mother and father.

Finding the Gift of the New Integration of Mother and Father

M: When you can see this symbol of synthesis and integration, very kindly and respectfully ask it, "What is the gift you have come all this way to give me?" And listen to the answer. What is the gift that this integration has come all this way to give you?

D: For instance, the father's gift of "safety" and the mother's gift of "unconditional love" may become "peace" when integrated together. The mother's gift of a "safe harbor" and the father's gift of "protection from pain" may combine to become "togetherness and unity with God." Some other gifts that have come up for participants at our Tools of the Spirit seminars include: "Joy," "Spirit," "Warmth," "The Strength to Speak Truth," "Wholeness," "Energy" and "Life."

Spreading the Gift of the Integration

M: Notice the image or symbol and its gift and say, "Thank you, I accept this gift, no strings attached." And if you have no objection, gently, slowly and with kindness, use your hands to bring this gift into your heart. Sweetly, bring it directly into your heart and breathe it into your body.

D: Feel it flowing into your heart and lungs, and into your bones, muscles and blood stream. As you do, you can experience a sense of rebirth.

M: Feel it spread throughout your body from the top of your head to the bottoms of your feet. Let it spread and flow as if all of the atoms and molecules of your body are breathing in this experience, as it goes deeper. Experience it as though your muscles and bones are being kissed and caressed from the inside of your body.

D: As you feel the gift spreading and deepening, lift your hands gently up to the base of your throat.

M: Touch the base of your throat, feeling the connection between this gift and your sense of self.

D: Bring the feeling of this wonderful gift into each of your cells and the marrow of your bones. And also begin to let it flow into your past. Take this feeling back in time, into your personal history.

M: Imagine you are becoming younger and younger, taking this feeling with you into your past. The gift, which is now in your heart and blood and bones, spreads throughout your life.

D: Feel yourself becoming younger and younger, all the way to the point just before you were born. Notice this gift is there within you in your mother's womb.

M: Go back to the moment of your conception, when your mother's egg and your father's sperm joined together. Notice that this feeling of integration is there.

D: Allow this feeling to go into the mother's egg.

M: And allow it to go into the father's sperm.

D: Through the egg, the feeling goes into your mother. Imagine the gift flowing into your mother's body through the egg.

M: And the gift goes through the sperm into your father's body.

D: It goes into your mother and your mother's mother.

M: And it goes into your father and your father's father.

D: The gift goes back farther and farther, into all the branches of your family history. Through the egg it goes to your mother's mother, and grandmother, and all the women in your lineage.

M: Through the sperm, the gift is transmitted to your father's father, and grandfather, and all the men in your lineage.

D: Bring the gift all the way back to your earliest ancestors, sensing that this gift has been in your history since the beginning of time. Then begin to come slowly back to the present. Feeling the gift being passed down from generation to generation. Each mother passes it to her daughters.

M: And each father passes it to his sons. The gift strengthens and deepens as it is handed down to each new generation. Feel it coming forward through your father's great grandfather, and his grandfather, and your father's father, to your father.

D: Feel the gift being passed down through your mother's great grandmother, and her grandmother, and your mother's mother, to your mother. And through the egg of your mother, the gift is given to you.

M: And it is there in the sperm of your father as it joins with the egg of your mother at your conception. Feel the integration as the sperm and the egg unite. And as you begin to grow, you double in size and double again, and the feeling doubles and doubles again within you.

D: This feeling of integration and wholeness continues to multiply and spread with each cell.

M: And you grow and grow until it's time for you to be born.

D: And you're born with this gift deeply within your heart and your blood and your bones.

M: Born into the night or the day, breathing, living, being, with this feeling spreading as you grow.

D: The gift fills your life as you grow through your first year and second year, becoming stronger each year.

M: Feel yourself growing up with this gift of integration in your heart. Bring it through your childhood and young adulthood, feeling it becoming stronger and deeper, until you are here and now with this feeling, knowing you've always had it.

D: It's always been here.

M: And it will continue through tomorrow and the next day, and the weeks, months, years and decades to come, spreading throughout your future in every direction.

D: Watch and feel it continue to unfold in your future, experiencing a deeper and deeper sense of wholeness and rebirth with each day.

M: Bring this experience of integration fully into your body as you sit here now.

D: Allow your hands to move back to your lap. Notice what your life will feel like from now on with this new integration totally inside of you. Be in the energy of the present with the new integration and the gift of your mother and father. And when you're ready, you can take a deep breath, feeling your body as you breathe.

Summary of the Self-Parenting Process
(The Archetype Patterns)

1. <u>Think about your mother, or The Mother,</u> and notice any feelings associated with her. Now notice where in your body your mother, or The Mother, resides. Where do you feel her living?

2. Intensify the feeling of your mother even more and allow the feeling to stream from its location in your body into the open palm of your left hand. The feeling flows into your left hand until all of the feeling is represented.

3. Now allow the feeling of your mother in your left hand to become an image you can see. If you could see it, what image does your mother take? Say to this image, "I asked you to come and you came. Thank you for coming.

4. Say to this image, "I'm going to turn my attention elsewhere, now. Please excuse me."

5. <u>Now, think about your father, or The Father,</u> and notice any feelings associated with him. Notice where in your body your father, or The Father, resides. Where do you feel him living?

6. Intensify the feeling of your father even more and allow the feeling to stream from its location into the open palm of your right hand. The feeling flows into your right hand until all of the feeling is represented.

7. Now allow the feeling of your father in your right hand to become an image you can see. If you could see it, what image does your father take? Say to this image, "I asked you to come and you came. Thank you for coming.

8. Say to this image, "I'm going to turn my attention elsewhere, now. Please excuse me."

9. Ask for the Meta-Outcomes from your Mother and Father: In turn, ask both your Mother and Father, "What is your positive purpose, the gift you are trying to give me?" Accept the gift 'with no strings attached,' and if you have a gift for each of them, give it 'with no strings attached.'

10. Now, ask your Mother and then your Father if they can understand and appreciate, in terms of their own intentions, the value and usefulness of the other parent's Meta-Outcome.

11. When both parents accept the other parent's Meta-Outcome as valuable, explain the need for them to work together in new and more effective ways.

12. Now, slowly bring both hands together. Watch and feel your Mother and Father meet, mix, mingle and merge together. (PAUSE) And now, open your hands to discover a new image which represents a full integration and synthesis. What was separate is now one. Ask, "What is the gift you have come to give me?"

13. If there is no objection, bring the gift, the integration image into your heart and breathe it into your lungs, your heart, your bones and your blood stream. Experience a sense of 'rebirth.'

14. Now touch the base of your throat to anchor this new integrated feeling.

15. As you touch your throat, let the feeling you have take you all the way into your past, to just before you were born. Be in your mother's womb feeling this way. As both sperm and egg, allow yourself to continue going back into all the branches of your family history. Now,

with this feeling deeply within your history, your body and your cellular structure, gently bring it back up through all the branches of your family and years of your life to this present moment. Watch it continue to gently unfold into your future. Experience a deeper sense of rebirth.

16. As you let go of the throat-anchor, notice what your life will feel like from now on with this integration totally within you.

part three

Rebirth

Symbolic Rebirth Cycle

Spiritual Renewal Process

Closing

Chapter 9

Symbolic Rebirth Cycle

Overview of Chapter 9

- Rebirth
- Silly Greetings
- Stories: A Tool to Celebrate Rebirth
- Mary And Joseph On Their Way to Bethlehem
- Cycles of Change
- Storytelling
- The Symbolic Rebirth Cycle (The Never Ending Story)
- Creating Your Symbols
- Telling Your Story
- Robert Dilts' Story
- Robert McDonald's Story
- Those Who Have Ears To Hear

Rebirth

D: Our theme for this section is "Rebirth." In previous sections we have aligned various levels of ourselves and integrated our perceptions of the present and eternity to give "Birth" to a sense of "spiritual wholeness." We have applied this sense of spiritual wholeness in the service of healing. We have also experienced that a spiritual awakening leads to a deeper awareness of the Shadow. By exploring the shadow and confronting "Death," we were able to let go of "that which is no longer necessary." This allows us the opportunity for the experience of "Rebirth."

In this section we will explore processes and tools related to the "Rebirth." For instance, one of the most common ways in which we acknowledge rebirth is through greetings. Greetings symbolize the 'rebirth' of our continuing relationship with others.

Silly Greetings

M: Around the world, when people greet each other, they typically say "Hello," or an equivalent. For example, in Germany people say, "Gut morgen". In Japan, people greet each other by saying, "Konichiwa." In Brazil people say, "Bon Dia."

D: When people greet each other, they also touch, shake hands, or do something physical, such as bowing or making eye contact.

M: Not all cultures touch or make eye contact. But if you hadn't experienced that culture before, you wouldn't know what was appropriate. You would have to pay attention. You'd have to notice the different ways people had of greeting each other.

I wonder if we didn't have a particular cultural way of greeting each other, what your individual way would be? For instance, if you were going to say "good morning" to somebody and couldn't use any words, but you could use sounds, movement or a touch, what would your greeting be?

D: You might create a reflection of how you were feeling in the moment. For example, I might say to Robert, "Ahhh." (Dilts opens his arms wide above his head.)

M: In order for me to return Robert's greeting, I'd do the same thing. I'd say, "Ahhh." (McDonald opens his arms wide above his head.)

Then I would give Robert my own greeting. I'd say, "Ooh, ooh, ooh." (McDonald rubs his stomach and pats his head, like a chimp.)

D: And I would return that greeting to Robert by saying, "Ooh, ooh, ooh." (Dilts rubs his stomach and pats his head, like a chimp.)

When we begin "Rebirth" day in our Tools of the Spirit Seminars, we often like to ask people to go around the room and greet each other with their own personal "silly" greetings.

M: The greeting can include words, or it can be completely nonverbal.

D: Two people face each other and one of them starts by making his or her greeting. That person's partner then greets him or her back in the same manner. Then, the second person gives his or her own silly greeting, which is returned by the other person. So they take turns matching one another.

M: These greetings are special, individual, and creative. We ask people to express their own sense of 'rebirth' by going around the room giving silly greetings and receiving them back.

Stories: A Tool to Celebrate Rebirth

D: One of the most common tools of the spirit, in addition to song, ritual, prayer and meditation, is storytelling. Parables, fables and metaphors are all forms of stories. It is important to keep in mind that stories are not just a recounting of an actual event. The meaning of a metaphor is not its surface structure. The deeper structure of the story carries its meaning. Spiritual stories in particular are symbolic rather than literal.

M: Have you ever had a dream during the night and, in the morning, you awakened feeling very good about the dream, but you didn't consciously know why? You have the feeling that something got resolved or transformed, but you're not sure what it was. And even though you remember things about the dream, you can't quite figure out how it could have led to the feeling of deep resolution, but somehow it did. It is as if a transformation has occurred in what Arnold and Amy Mindell call "the dream body."

Mary And Joseph On Their Way to Bethlehem

D: Gregory Bateson used to give the example of a particular British hymn about Mary and Joseph on their way to Bethlehem for the census. Mary was 'great with child' and tired of traveling. She began complaining to her husband about being very tired and hungry. So they pulled the donkey over and stopped by the side of the road. Mary, who had become a bit irritable from their long journey, said to Joseph, "I'm hungry, would you pick me some cherries from that cherry tree over there?" Joseph who was also a little tired and irritable, and not too happy about having to stop, responded, "Let the one who got you pregnant get you the cherry." About that time, the cherry tree bent over and offered Mary a cherry from its branches.

Gregory points out that if you say, "Wait a minute, there were no cherry trees in Palestine in the first century," you have missed the purpose of the story. Its like asking, "What happened to the monk after he ate the strawberry?" in Robert's story. To take the story literally will rob it of its deeper meaning. The literal interpretation obscures the intention of the story. In other words, when Jesus talked about a sower planting seeds, he wasn't really intending to give a lecture on gardening. Rather there was a symbolic nature to the story. Understanding and creating a tool of the spirit requires the ability, as Robert said, to feel, work and think in that language of dreams and symbols. The language of the spirit is necessarily a nonliteral language. What is sacred is not in what is literal but what is found in the deeper structure.

Cycles of Change

D: In this section we will present two processes relating to rebirth. The first one is something that we call the *Symbolic Rebirth Cycle*. It is based on a belief change technique that I developed, which is known by several different names: The Thought Inoculation Process, The Belief Change Cycle (see *Strategies of Genius Volume III*, 1995) and the Walking Belief Change Process. Robert McDonald has an excellent videotape on the Walking Belief Change Process (NLP Comprehensive, 1994). The Symbolic Rebirth Cycle is based on the premise that all change and growth, including spiritual growth, occurs around fundamental cycles - such as birth, death and rebirth.

M: How many of you have had experiences of rebirth? I have had a few. For example, I used to believe that I was "stupid." At a certain point when I was growing up, however, I had enough evidence of being intelligent that

there was a shift inside of me. I experienced a type of
"rebirth." And the interesting thing was that, in order to
believe that I was "intelligent," I had to let go of the belief
that I was "stupid." My limiting belief had to "die" and be
put in its proper place.

In my family, we all seemed to 'aspire to mediocrity'. I
grew up believing it was necessary to never stand out. In
fact, in my family, to stand out was to invite more pain. I
was the only one in my family to finish college and
graduate school, and that meant letting go of a whole
other way of being. But in that death came the birth of a
new way for me, and also a rebirth in the way my family
related to me.

Similarly, some people think the world is essentially
evil. But when a transformation, or "rebirth" occurs, the
world becomes a glorious, beautiful, place in which God is
always present.

I have often worked with people who are suicidal. My
personal experience of my father's suicide helps me to
relate to people in that type of struggle. People who are
suicidal feel that they need to die in order to solve or avoid
their problems. I believe there is some truth to that
feeling, but that it is being taken on the wrong level.
What I notice is that clearly *something* needs to die, it just
isn't the person's body. It is not the body that needs to die.
What needs to die is the person's lifestyle - the way he or
she has been living. Of course, there are some people who
say, "I'd rather kill my body than change my lifestyle."
What they need is a way to transform their beliefs, to
have a rebirth. They need a way to be born again
spiritually, mentally and emotionally. They need a way to
be renewed. They need to discover that the perception
that the glass is 'half empty' creates an entire world. And
the perception that the glass is 'half full' creates another
world. Shifting that perception is a type of symbolic
rebirth.

D: Another way of thinking about what we mean by "Rebirth" is in terms of our life cycles. When you're a child you go through a number of developmental cycles. I have watched my own children go through several cycles in which they leave and enter different stages of their lives. They leave being an infant to become a toddler, and then they transform from a toddler to a child. A child eventually becomes an adolescent, and so on. In each of those stages of change there is a kind of "death" and "rebirth." I think even very young children recognize that.

I remember when my daughter was first becoming toilet trained. She had essentially toilet trained herself by the age of 18 months. Perhaps it was because she had an older brother, but she toilet trained herself very early. And suddenly, I think she had an intuition that toilet training wasn't just a behavior. It was a symbol of leaving behind her infancy and going on to become a toddler. At that point she started having a lot of accidents. She started regressing, and began wetting her pants and her bed again for a while. It wasn't because she lost the capability of controlling herself. In fact, she started to say to my wife and I, "Carry me like a baby". I think that somewhere within her, she was not yet ready to let go of being a baby. She needed to be willing to let go of that stage before she could be reborn as a toddler.

We have all had experiences of rebirth. Perhaps it was letting go of an old job and transitioning to a new job, or ending one relationship in order to start a new one. These are different types of rebirth.

Every time Robert and I do *Tools of the Spirit* there's also a kind of a rebirth. There's a death of the old *Tools of the Spirit* program, and a rebirth of the new one. And if we didn't have that rebirth, the seminar would become stale. It would become a hollow ritual, rather than a ritual in which the miracle might happen.

Birth, death and rebirth are like the changing seasons. "Birth" is the Springtime when the new grass is growing and the seeds are sprouting. The seeds of a spiritual quest typically come in the form of a yearning for greater spiritual contact or wholeness. People long for some form of guidance, peace, freedom, love or healing. The Spring-time of this spiritual quest involves becoming open to spiritual awakening. The Sacred Journey process, for example, is about opening to the awakening of spirit. We bring more of the sense of spiritual wholeness into our bodies and relationships through processes such as the Presence of Eternity and Spiritual Healing.

This is like the transition from Spring to Summer. The seeds which started as a yearning for more spiritual wholeness begin to grow and mature. But the attempt to bring more of our larger "S" self into being also brings us in contact with our Shadow. The heat of the Summer sun brings new challenges. Some of the green grass begins to wither and die. As long as "spiritual wholeness" is just an idea and a dream, we don't have to face our Shadows. If the "spiritual" stays in the realm of fantasy, then it can be all "cotton candy and ice cream." But when you attempt to bring it into reality, you must confront your Shadow.

Autumn is the time of opening to letting go of that which is no longer necessary. That's what the Releasing Enmeshment With The Shadow process is all about. Opening to the Shadow, finding the Shadow, and finally opening to letting go of that which is no longer necessary. In a way it is like the harvest time. The releasing enmeshment process is a type of harvesting. You sort out the grain from the shell, the wheat from the chaff. You are sorting out that which is no longer necessary, and main-taining the fruit, the meat, for yourself.

Then there's the Wintertime. The season of the winter involves honoring the place of the Shadow. The Winter snow covers everything. Everything that is not needed has been released. You've reached the stage of maturity and are waiting for the next phase. What's next? A new yearning, and the coming of the next Spring.

People often wonder how it is possible for Robert and I to still have Shadows to work with. What we need to realize is that as long as there's a Spring, there's going to be another harvest and another Winter. And the Winter is going to lead to a Spring. That is the "never-ending" story. It is a story that has been told and retold since time immemorial.

We have all had many experiences of rebirth in our lives, many stories of rebirth. "Tools of the Spirit" is also a story, and if you had no story to tell at this stage in your evolution, we would not have been successful. The Symbolic Rebirth process is about telling stories. You are going to tell the story of the spiritual rebirth you have been experiencing throughout your exploration of "Tools of the Spirit."

We are going to create these stories by finding images or symbols for the different states that make up the cycle of spiritual rebirth:

Yearning for spiritual wholeness
Opening to spiritual awakening
Embodying more spiritual wholeness
Opening to letting go of the unnecessary, and
Honoring the proper place of the Shadow.

At the center of this eternal cycle of change is a "sacred space" around which the whole process revolves.

Storytelling

M: Storytelling itself is a fascinating process. Think of a time you told a story to a child. Have you ever been right in the middle of the story and didn't know where it was going next? But you told it anyway? And the child was thrilled with what you said. When you start to tell the story and let it lead you, it takes on a life of its own. It's similar to painting or drawing. If you have a certain canvas or page, after awhile, it paints itself. It lets you know what's next. It lets you know how to complete it. Many people think that they can't tell stories. But when they start off with the words "once upon a time," it is a signal to the unconscious mind. The words "once upon a time" are a secret code that says, "It's okay now to open the unconscious mind and allow transformations to occur at much deeper levels." When you allow that to occur, you can tell any story.

D: Telling a story is also a little like creating a play. You have a stage, a landscape, and in the telling of the story you act it out. If you ever watch the way children tell stories, they don't just sit there and tell it, they act it. Sometimes telling a story is a little bit like an impromptu play.

M: In order to do that, you need to build a stage and gather some characters.

D: The final step is to create the dialog.

The Symbolic Rebirth Cycle
(The Never Ending Story)

The symbolic rebirth cycle involves creating symbols for each of the states that make up the 'landscape' of spiritual rebirth. The symbols are then synthesized into a personal story or metaphor for rebirth.

When coming up with the symbols, it is important to keep in mind that they do not need to 'logically' relate to each other in any way. They should just simply emerge from your unconscious. It is not necessary that they make any sense at first. Just write down what pops into your mind as a symbol for the state.

Remember that the states which make up the cycle and their symbols should be kept general and do not need to be connected to any particular situation. This process also involves the use of your symbols for your big 'S' Self and the 'Shadow'. As an analogy, the symbols relating to the states which make up the rebirth cycle represent the 'stage' on which the story is played out. The large 'S' Self and the 'Shadow' are the 'characters' that move around on that stage.

In preparation for this process, create a "landscape" for spiritual rebirth. On the floor, establish the following five locations, representing the cycle of spiritual transformation, in the form of a large ring or circle:

Yearning for spiritual wholeness
Opening to spiritual awakening
Currently embodying
Opening to letting go of the unnecessary
Honoring the Shadow's proper place

In the center of the circle, establish a sixth space that is a 'Sacred Space' for trusting in a higher spiritual power.

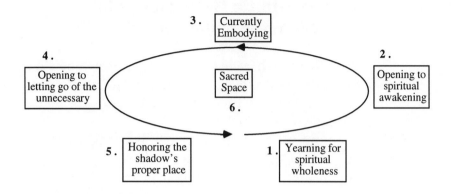

"Landscape" for Spiritual Transformation

One of the "characters" in the story will be the large "S" Self that you drew a picture of in the section on "Birth." Another character in the story will be your "Shadow." Use the symbol for your Shadow that you created during the Releasing Enmeshment process.

The following Worksheet summarizes the steps we will be following in order to create the remaining symbols which will be synthesized into the story.

Symbolic Rebirth Worksheet

1. Stand into the 'Yearning for spiritual wholeness' space and think of what it is like when you deeply desire spiritual wholeness. Create a symbol or metaphor for 'Yearning for spiritual wholeness'.
   e.g. 'Light reflecting off of a drop of dew'.

Your symbol: _____

2. Write down the metaphor or symbol that you have created for your large 'S' Self.
   e.g. 'Christmas tree made of light.'

Your symbol: _____

3. Move into the 'Opening to spiritual awakening' space and think of what it is like when you are open to an awakening or renewal on a spiritual level. What is your metaphor or symbol for 'opening to spiritual awakening'?
   e.g. 'Beam of light shining into the heart'.

Your symbol: _____

4. Stand in the 'Currently embodying' space and think of your small 's' self. Create a symbol or metaphor for the small 's' self you are currently embodying.
   e.g. 'Thread about to break'.

Your symbol: _____

5. Write down the metaphor or symbol that you have discovered for your 'Shadow'.
   e.g. 'A dark fog'.

Your symbol: _____

6. Move into the 'Opening to letting go of the unnecessary' space and think of a time you were ready to let go of something that you had been holding onto for a long time. What is your metaphor or symbol for 'opening to letting go of the unnecessary'?

　　e.g. *'Water cleansing the body and flowing through the gateway of the heart'.*

Your symbol: _____

7. Stand in the 'Honoring the shadow's proper place' space (your "museum of personal history") and remember something you used to be a part of your life or identity that is now a part of your history but not your identity. What is your metaphor or symbol for the 'shadows' that you have transformed?

　　e.g. *'Skeletons in a museum'.*

Your symbol: _____

8. Step into the 'Sacred Space'. Create a symbol or metaphor for the experience of trusting in something beyond yourself.

　　e.g. *'Sky and clouds on the horizon'.*

Your symbol: _____

You already have some of these symbols (the large "S" Self and the Shadow). The others we will need to create. And the way that you create the symbols is by starting from a feeling. You start from the internal feeling state associated with a particular part of the cycle, and let the symbol emerge naturally from the feeling.

Creating Your Symbols

Yearning for Spiritual Wholeness

D: The first symbol is that of the "yearning for spiritual wholeness." This relates to the desire for greater spiritual connection or guidance in your life. To create my symbol, I would stand in the space on the landscape marked "yearning for spiritual wholeness" and think of what it is like when I deeply desire spiritual connection or guidance.

M: As Robert thinks about what's it like when he deeply desires spiritual wholeness, he notices the feeling associated with that state of yearning. When he is able to feel what it is like when he has had a deep desire for spiritual wholeness, Robert allows the feeling to become an image or a symbol.

D: For me the symbol that naturally emerges is a satellite antenna pointing toward the night sky.

M: So Robert would write down "satellite antenna pointing to the night sky" in the space provided at **step 1** on the Symbolic Rebirth Worksheet.

M: When I get into the state of yearning for spiritual wholeness and discover what image comes, I see a flower turning its face towards the sun.

D: So Robert's symbol is a flower turning its face towards the sun. That's what he would write down in the space at **step 1**.

Try this for yourself. You can do it either sitting or standing. Recall your own experiences of yearning for spiritual wholeness. What do you feel when you deeply desire spiritual wholeness?. It may be the desire for inner peace, healing, congruence, commitment or love.

M: There have been times in your life when you've had great yearning for spiritual wholeness. Notice what this feels like in your body now. Touch the part of your body where you most strongly feel this sensation. Then let the feeling become a symbol or an image you can see. If this feeling of yearning for spiritual wholeness could become a symbol or image you could see, what would it be?

D: If it helps, you can start the sentence, "My feeling of yearning for spiritual wholeness is like..." and notice whatever phrase, symbol or image spontaneously emerges. What would it be?

M: As soon as you notice it, write it down in the space at **step 1** on the worksheet.

D: Some examples of symbols and images for the state of yearning for spiritual wholeness that have come up for people in our *Tools of the Spirit* seminars include:

> A box with sides of light, spinning in space.
> The beginning of a long trip home.
> A fledgling bird watching its parents fly, and wanting to go with them.
> Going towards the light at the end of a tunnel.
> An archer shooting an arrow toward a rainbow
> The smell of an ancient forest and the longing for light.

Your Large "S" Self

M: The symbol for step number 2 is one that you already have. It's the drawing that you made of your capital "S" Self. Just write down a brief description of the metaphor or symbol that you created for your large "S" Self.

D: For example, I would write down "a magic wand with colorful streams of light."

M: And I would write down "a radiant body with face unfolding; like an artichoke." Write down your symbol in the space at **step 2**.

Opening to Spiritual Awakening

D: The next symbol is for the state of "opening to spiritual awakening."

M: To access this state you would recall what it's like to be open to the awakening and renewal of your spirit. When you have a felt sense of being open to renewing your spirit, notice what image or symbol emerges.

D: The symbol that emerges for me, for example, is the beak of a baby bird cracking through the shell of its egg. That is what I would write in the space at **step 3**.

M: My image is of myself on my knees with my head bowed, in a state of surrender.

To find your own symbol, think of what it's like when you're open to an awakening or renewal of the spirit. Notice what you feel when you are truly open to a renewal of your spirit. Touch the part of your body where you most strongly feel this sensation, and let the feeling become a symbol or an image you can see.

D: Start the sentence, "My feeling of opening to spiritual awakening is like..." and notice whatever phrase, symbol or image spontaneously emerges. If the feeling of opening to spiritual awakening could become a symbol or image you could see, what would it be?

M: Whatever symbol comes to your mind, that's the one. Write it down in the space at **step 3**. Here are some examples of symbols for the state of opening to spiritual awakening from people in our Tools of the Spirit seminars.

A large red flower in full bloom with very light rain falling.

A white staircase surrounded by white puffy clouds.
Water flowing over a rock.
A person on her knees with her head bowed and a shaft
of white light shining through top of the head all the
way down the spine.
Pats of melting butter.
A leap of faith through a window of light.

Currently Embodying - The Small "s" Self

D: The next symbol is for the self that we are "currently
embodying." This is essentially our current small "s" self.
Earlier, Robert McDonald spoke about his dream of being
the bird, and knowing that this was his true self. Yet, in
order to embody that bird, he had to come down onto the
planet and bring it into his physical body. The larger "S"
Self had to come into being through the smaller "s" self, a
self that is limited in time and space. Our next symbol
represents our current small "s" self.

To find the symbol, stand in the "currently embodying"
space on the landscape and think of your small "s" self -
your physical, mundane self.

M: This is you as a limited, finite, mundane being. Put
yourself fully into the feeling state of being in your small
"s" self and notice what image or symbol emerges.

D: The image that immediately comes up for me is a bundle
of sticks tied together.

M: Mine came immediately as well. It's a wooden person, a
wooden Indian.

D: Remember that the small "s" self is not your Shadow, it's
the everyday mundane you. Take a moment and think of
what it's like when you are in your small "s" self. Get into
the feeling sense of being the everyday you. Touch the
part of your body where you most strongly feel this

sensation, and let the feeling become a symbol or an image you can see.

M: Start the sentence, "My small "s" self is like..." and notice whatever phrase, symbol or image spontaneously emerges. If the feeling associated with your little "s" self could become a symbol or image you could see, what would it be? Allow an image or a symbol to emerge from your sense of the 'mundane you', the everyday you. When you have this symbol, write it down in the space provided at **step 4** on the Symbolic Rebirth Worksheet.

D: Here are some symbols that have emerged for people in our Tools of the Spirit seminars.

> The ball in a pinball machine.
> A wooden block.
> Sitting in a dark closet.
> Three horizontal ovals in a triangular shape.
> Being closed up in a box.
> Leaves laying on the ground of a forest.
> A tin man.
> A closed locked safe made of ice.

The Shadow

M: In the space provided at **step 5** on the Symbolic Rebirth Worksheet write down the symbol or image that you discovered for your "Shadow" during the Opening to the Shadow process.

D: Mine, for example, was a mass of slimy fibers coming from a bunch of kelp.

M: Mine was a like puddle of black ink, but instead of being a regular puddle it's upright. Its 3-dimensional black ink. Some other examples from participants at our Tools of the Spirit seminars have included:

An encased heart.
A little girl with fangs standing in a doorway.
Hands grabbing the throat.
A spike through the heart.
Dark boiling clouds.
A black snake going up the spine.

Opening to Letting Go of the Unnecessary

D: The next symbol to be incorporated into our story of rebirth relates to the state of "opening to letting go of that which is no longer necessary."

M: To get this symbol, think about times in your life when you had been holding onto something very tightly, and then began to realize you no longer needed it. It was OK to let it go. Put yourself into the feeling of those times in your life, and allow a symbol or image to come to mind of being open to let go of the unnecessary.

D: The image that emerges for me is a dark metal cable transforming into a beam of light.

M: For me it's my heart bulging and then just beginning to open up and let go of something it's been hanging onto. It is as if there has been a scar or a wound that my heart has been holding onto, but now I'm beginning to notice that I can let go of it. It's no longer necessary to keep it in my heart.

D: Robert and I would write down these symbols in the space provided at **step 6** of the Symbolic Rebirth Worksheet.

Take some time and find your own symbol for the state of opening to letting go of the unnecessary. For instance, you might remember what it felt like after you had created the image of your spiritually evolving self and asked for the positive intention of your enmeshment with the Shadow. That was a time when you became open to letting go of your Shadow. You opened to let go of that which was no longer necessary.

M: It's interesting to hold onto something for a long long time and realize how painful it can be. And then there comes a time when you realize you are ready to release it, because you no longer need it. Get into the feeling sense of opening to letting go of the unnecessary. Touch the part of your body where you most strongly feel this sensation, and let the feeling become a symbol or an image you can see.

D: Start the sentence, "The feeling of opening to letting go of the unnecessary is like..." and notice whatever phrase, symbol or image spontaneously emerges. If the feeling associated with opening to letting go of the unnecessary could become a symbol or image you could see, what would it be?

M: What do you see? As you know what it is, write it down in the space at **step 6**.

Here are some examples from our Tools of the Spirit participants:

A torrential rainstorm.
Sunlight like diamonds on the water in a storm.
A crab with little pinchers.
A child opening her hands.
A ball being dropped from a skyscraper.
Emptying a dusty old chest.
A big lake of bright blue water.

Honoring the Shadow's Proper Place - The Museum of Personal History

D: The next symbol is for the state of "honoring the Shadow's proper place." This relates to what I like to call "the museum of personal history." In an actual museum, we see the clothing, tools, weapons, art and other remains of our ancestors. We acknowledge and honor these artifacts as a part of our history, but we also recognize that they are no longer a key aspect of our current way of dressing, working or being. Muskets, chamber pots and Model T's are no longer a necessary part of modern life. Your "museum of personal history" is a place where you can remember incidents and events that are a part of your history, but are no longer a part of your identity. They are no longer relevant to the way you currently think, behave or relate to others.

In this case, you want to find a symbol for having completed the process of letting go of the Shadow. It is your image for honoring the Shadow's proper place; the emotional experience that you have with respect to things that are no longer a part of your life. Find your symbol for the experience of recalling Shadows that used to limit you but now have no impact on you.

The image that emerges for me for honoring the Shadow's proper place, for instance, is a stream or a river flowing into a bay at dusk.

M: My symbol is a graveyard or cemetery, with many headstones in the shape of a cross. This is what I would write down in the space at **step 7**.

D: At the completion of the process of Releasing Enmeshment with the Shadow, you released or let go of your Shadow, and put it in its proper place. That shadow had played a significant role in your life. When it became connected to its own spiritual essence, however, it was able to be in its own proper place. By connecting yourself to your own spiritual essence and seeing your shadow connected to its own spiritual essence, you were able to honor the Shadow's proper place.

As you recall that experience, notice the emotional state you feel. Think of some other Shadows, beliefs or blocks that used to be a part of your life but which no longer limit you. Perhaps you can think of some of those experiences in which you can 'forgive and remember'. Notice the feeling you have in relationship to previous blocks and limitations that you can remember, but which you know are not a part of your life anymore.

M: Touch the part of your body where you most strongly feel this sensation, and let the feeling become a symbol or an image you can see.

D: Start the sentence, "The feeling of honoring the Shadow's proper place is like..." and notice whatever phrase, symbol or image spontaneously emerges. If the feeling associated with honoring the proper place of the Shadow could become a symbol or image you could see, what would it be?

M: When you have the image, write it down in the space at **step 7** on the Symbolic Rebirth Worksheet. Some examples from our Tools of the Spirit participants include:

A highflying kite connected by a string but which has a lot of freedom to fly.
A filing cabinet filled with old files.
Smoke from an extinguishing fire.
A room filled with the portraits of ancestors.
A display case of mummies.
An asteroid out in the solar system.

Sacred Space

D: The last symbol making up our story of rebirth involves what we call the "Sacred Space." The space for this symbol is at the center of the cycle of change. The "Sacred Space" relates to the experience of trusting in something beyond yourself, or being in the presence of the spiritual. It is your personal experience of the sacred, of what it is like when you have a sense of contact with "spirit," "source," "God" or "universe." It may be very similar to your state of spiritual wholeness.

M: It is your felt experience of "faith," or trusting in something beyond yourself.

D: The symbol that comes up for me of my sacred space is looking out into the universe and seeing a blanket of very distant stars.

M: As I go into that experience and feel my body, the symbol that comes up for me is Christ standing behind me, touching my shoulders.

D: So, just as Robert and I have done, you can recall experiences in which you were able to have a sense of faith or contact with something beyond yourself - something which is inherently good, friendly and healing.

M: You might start by asking yourself, "Have I ever felt safe? Have I ever felt trusting? Have I ever just relaxed and been held?" For instance, have you ever been in the forest and put your head down by a tree and allowed the tree to support you? Have you ever been lying down on a hammock and trusted that the world would not shake so much that you would be knocked out of it? Have you ever been in a turmoil in the midst of a family fight in the kitchen and known that things were all right and you were safe? Have you ever been in the presence of death and dying and known that somehow there's something that goes beyond all appearances? Have you ever known that safety? That place of sacredness? Take this feeling and go to all the other times that you've had it. And then you can allow this feeling and the multitudes of these experiences to become an image or a symbol representing the sacred place or feeling of trust.

D: Touch the part of your body where you most strongly feel this sensation, and let the feeling become a symbol or an image you can see. Start the sentence, "The feeling associated with my sacred space is like..." and notice whatever phrase, symbol or image spontaneously emerges. If the feeling associated with your sacred space could become a symbol or image you could see, what would it be? When you have it, write it down in the space at **step 8**.

M: Here are some examples of symbols which have emerged for participants at our Tools of the Spirit seminars.

A tiny embryo.
Walking in a dark tunnel, completely fearless.
A firmly established lighthouse on the rocks.
A huge stained glass window with the outstretched hands of Jesus.
A burning bush.
A leap of faith into the hand of God.
A toddler holding onto the hand of his or her father.
The sun beam shining through the heart.
The stone floor of a temple.

Telling Your Story

D: We have now generated quite an assortment of symbols. I'm sure that some of your conscious minds are considering all of these symbols and wondering how on earth you are going to make them into a story. I know that when my conscious mind looks at all these symbols and images it thinks, "Satellite dish pointing to the sky, a magic wand with stream of colors, a baby bird breaking out of an egg, a bundle of sticks, a mass of slimy fibers, metal cable becoming a beam of light, a stream flowing into an ocean at dusk and a blanket of stars; how do I make a story out of all of that?" Fortunately, my conscious mind doesn't have to make the story out of them. My unconscious mind is going to weave these symbols into a story. Remember, this is not the kind of story that needs to follow a logical progression. You simply start with the words, "Once upon a time," and let the story begin to flow.

Now, if you are going to tell a story, you need to tell it to someone. In our Tools of the Spirit seminars, people simply form small groups of 4 or 5 and tell their stories to one another. If you are not able to find another person or group to talk to, you can write your story. In this case, you may want to imagine you are talking to an audience. Tell the story in your head as if you were talking to a group, and then write down what comes to your mind.

Who you mentally select as audience members is important because they will influence how you tell the story. Earlier, Robert asked whether you'd ever told a story to a child. It is also interesting to recall what it is like to listen to a child's story. My children are at an age at which they like to tell stories. When I listen to the stories of my children, I don't listen to them the same way I would read literature in a college English class. I'm not thinking about the fine points of style or grammar. I listen with ears that say, "I'm ready, I'm listening, I want to hear whatever you have to say." So, if you are going to tell your story mentally, imagine that you are talking to people who have that type of attitude.

When someone is telling a story, the state of the listeners helps to draw out the creativity of the storyteller. When the members of an audience are sitting like children with their eyes wide and ready for anything, it is as if they are saying, "Tell me the story and I'll get something out of it. That's what I want. My heart is open. My spirit is open. My imagination is open. Tell me your story." That's also the way you want to listen to the stories of others. It involves listening for the deeper structure.

M: Before you start telling your story, put yourself into the proper mood. Become a storyteller, telling a story of spiritual rebirth. Realize that as you are telling your story, you don't have to tell it in the order in which the

symbols emerged. Instead of starting with your symbol for
yearning for spiritual wholeness, for instance, you could
start with your symbol for your small "s" self or the sacred
space.

I like to physically walk through the "change landscape" and stop in each particular location while I am
telling that part of the story.

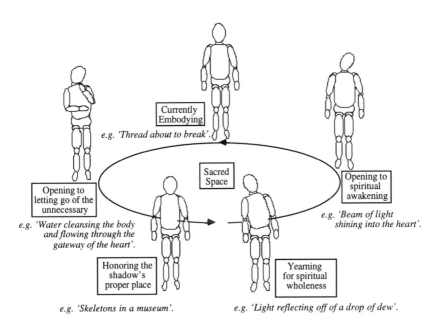

Walking Through the Cycle of Spiritual Change

D: To remember the symbols that you need to weave into
your story, you can either keep the Symbolic Rebirth
Worksheet in front of you, or if you are with a group, ask
one of the listeners to remind you of the symbols as you
intuitively move through the landscape of the cycle of
rebirth.

Here are the stories that Robert and I came up with,
using the symbols we discovered.

Robert Dilts' Story

Robert Dilts' Symbols:

Yearning for spiritual wholeness: <u>Satellite dish pointing to the sky</u>

Large "S" self: <u>A magic wand with streams of color</u>

Opening to spiritual awakening: <u>The beak of a baby bird breaking out of an egg</u>

Currently embodying (small "s" self): <u>A bundle of sticks</u>

The Shadow: <u>A mass of slimy fibers</u>

Opening to letting go of the unnecessary: <u>A metal cable becoming a beam of light</u>

Honoring the Shadow's proper place: <u>A stream flowing into an ocean at dusk</u>

Sacred space: <u>A blanket of distant stars</u>

Once upon a time there was a great blanket of stars. This blanket of stars covered and embraced the entire universe. It wanted very much to create a space of safety for all of the planets within its reach so that many different forms of life could emerge and grow freely. The blanket sent a gift to all of the tiny planets mixed in with the stars that it held in its embrace. To each planet, the blanket of stars sent a magic wand.

One particular magic wand was sent to a small blue and green planet. It was a very special wand that emanated many streams of color. It had magical powers that came from the love and the warmth of the blanket of stars. The colors that streamed from the wand had the magic of healing and could transform ugliness into beauty and illness into health. The wand pursued its mission with passion, bringing beauty and healing to as many areas of the blue and green planet as it could touch. The more transformation it produced, the more confident and proud the magic wand became of its abilities.

As the magic wand focused more and more on its work, however, it began to forget that the source of its magical colors was the blanket of distant stars. Without this awareness and connection, the streams of color began to grow dimmer. The wand had to work harder and harder to produce its transforming magic, eventually losing all contact with the blanket of stars from which it had come. As the streams of color became dimmer, they began to turn into dark slimy fibers, and the wand turned into a bundle of sticks. The slimy fibers encircled the bundle of sticks like a metal cable, making it tight and stiff. The bundle of sticks laid lifeless on the ground for a long time and darkness fell over the land. Many people became sick because the healing powers of the wand had been lost.

Then, one day, a heavy rain came and washed the bundle of sticks into a stream. The sticks floated down the stream for many miles, finally reaching the ocean just as the sun was about to set. The waves gently pushed the bundle of sticks onto the beach, washing away the slime from the fibers which had been holding the sticks together.

After a while, a child came walking by and found the bundle of sticks. He had been sent out to play by himself because his mother was very sick. The boy was lonely and wished very much that his mother would get well. He picked up the bundle of sticks and said to himself, "I'm going to play a game. I'm going to pretend that this old bundle of sticks is a magic wand." About that time, the boy saw a bird's egg sitting cold and alone on some rocks. He felt sorry for the egg because it was all by itself and had no mother. Waving the bundle of sticks over the abandoned egg, the boy looked up into the starry night sky and wished with all his heart that he could help the baby bird within the egg. He opened his arms wide like a satellite dish pointing to the sky.

All of a sudden, the beak of a baby bird began to break through the shell of the egg. As each piece of the shell fell away, the cable holding the bundle of sticks began to loosen and the fibers began to regain their color, eventually becoming brilliant streams of light. The boy's hope and imagination had transformed the bundle of sticks back into a magic wand. The colorful streams of light emanated out from the wand bringing health and beauty back into the world. And when the boy arrived home, he found to his joy that his mother was getting well.

The wand returned to its healing work with a power greater than ever. But every night, when it was done with its work, the magic wand turned into a perch for the little bird. The bird sat on the wand and sang a beautiful song to the night sky, and the wand never again forgot about the blanket of stars from which it had come.

That's my story. (Applause.)

The fact is that, as I was telling that story, there were times when I didn't know where it was going to go next. Then suddenly, I would get an idea. I didn't know about the child, for instance when I started this story. I knew about the symbols, but I didn't know how they would all fit together. That is what we mean when we say to just allow the story to tell itself.

Robert McDonald's Story

Robert McDonald's Symbols:

Yearning for spiritual wholeness: <u>A flower turning its face toward the sun</u>

Large "S" self: <u>A radiant body with face unfolding; like an artichoke</u>

Opening to spiritual awakening: <u>A person on his knees with head bowed in a state of surrender</u>

Currently embodying (small "s" self): <u>A wooden Indian</u>

The Shadow: <u>A 3-dimensional puddle of black ink</u>

Opening to letting go of the unnecessary: <u>A heart opening up to let go of something</u>

Honoring the Shadow's proper place: <u>A graveyard with many headstones in the shape of a cross</u>

Sacred space: <u>Christ standing nearby, touching my shoulders</u>

Before telling my story, I like to walk around to each of the locations in the symbolic landscape and get a sense of them. This helps me to get a feeling for the general drift my story might take. (McDonald steps to the various locations representing the cycle of spiritual transformation. He stops at the space marked "currently embodying.")

Once upon a time there was a wooden Indian. He was very stiff, tall and proud. He stood silently and stiffly in the showcase next to the cigar store. He spent his days thinking that this kind of existence was what life was all about. There wasn't a lot going on inside of him.

Then, one day, an interesting thing happened to him. A black ink-like puddle appeared in front of him. The wooden Indian noticed the puddle, and was frightened. But at the same time he felt drawn to the puddle. The

Indian didn't know whether to lean away from it or lean toward it. He didn't know what was going to happen. Was he going to go into it, or was he going to back away?

Then something miraculous happened. A flower bud began to emerge from his forehead. As it emerged from his forehead it started to turn him toward the sun. But as he turned, the wooden Indian started to teeter and fell into the puddle of black ink. The next thing he knew, he found himself emerging from the other side of the puddle into a graveyard. He was now stained completely black. And the puddle of black ink had been transformed into one of the many gravestones, which were in the form of a cross.

The Indian stood there in this place of death, feeling not quite alive. The graveyard was so different from his showcase by the cigar store. Confused and disoriented, the wooden Indian began to walk through the graveyard. As he did, he suddenly noticed somebody on his knees, in a state of complete surrender. In the presence of the kneeling person, the stiff, ink stained wooden Indian found himself becoming so shaky that he actually fell to his own knees. The wooden Indian's knees had never been able to bend before.

As the wooden Indian adopted the posture of the kneeling person, something began to open up inside of him. It was his heart. His heart opened and out of it fell something he'd been carrying a long time. It was something old and yet he felt it was so precious that it had kept him wooden. He realized he had been holding on to this old memory, this old unfinished memory, for what seemed like an eternity. It was like a mass of sap that was stuck inside of him. But the more the Indian was on his knees, and the more that the flower blossomed from his forehead, the more his heart was able to open. As his heart continued to open wider, the sap rolled out into the graveyard, and he suddenly felt Christ's hands touch him on the shoulders.

The Indian couldn't believe what was happening, so he listened for a voice to guide him. As he knelt there listening, with the touch of Christ's hands on his shoulders, his whole head became like the blossoming flower. His head began to open like the petals of an artichoke. As the petals opened wider, the black ink became like a radiant body of light emerging from the wooden Indian. Suddenly he heard the words, "You are forgiven." At that moment, something deep inside of him was released and the light could come fully through his body. He heard the voice of Christ saying, "It's always been this way." But because the petals of the artichoke had opened his face, he could hear it for the first time.

And ever after, in his heart, he had a place that was so open that whatever came into it was transformed and could go out again. The wooden Indian was transformed into a being of radiant light, and wherever he visited, his touch and the love from his open heart had a healing power, a power that wasn't his but which was able to flow through his open heart. The end. (Applause.)

Those Who Have Ears To Hear

D: So, now it's time for you to tell your stories, and to listen with the ears of children to the stories of others. At our *Tools of the Spirit* seminar, we usually like to have people get into groups of about 4 or 5 and tell the stories. The stories are usually 5 to 10 minutes apiece.

Tell your story of 'rebirth' or 'transformation' by incorporating all of the metaphors and symbols that you have created. If you want to, as you are telling the story, you may physically walk to the spaces to which you are referring. You may also want to ask a member of your group to hold your Symbolic Rebirth Worksheet and remind you of your symbols as you are walking through your "landscape."

M: Allow the story to 'self-organize' itself. That is, be intuitive. Just begin and let the story take you where 'it needs to go'. Tell it as if you were telling a fairy tale to a child or as if it were a dream.   All you have to do is start with "Once upon a time" and let your unconscious mind do the rest. Just tell what emerges.   Trust your unconscious mind. It will tell the story.

Chapter 10

Spiritual Renewal

Overview of Chapter 10

- Life Landscapes
- Getting New Perspectives on Your Life
- Generative Change
- Spiritual Renewal: Tending Your Garden
- Demonstration of the Spiritual Renewal Process
- Steps of the Spiritual Renewal Process

Life Landscapes

D: Our final exercise for Tools of the Spirit is a process that we call *"Spiritual Renewal."* This process is based on my work in "Generative NLP" applications and the "Unified Field Theory for NLP." It involves laying out another type of "landscape." This is done by creating a grid intersecting "perceptual positions" with "time lines."

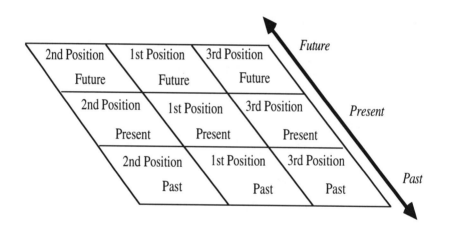

Spiritual Renewal Grid
(Generative NLP)

M: As with the Symbolic Rebirth Cycle, these spaces may be laid out on the floor.

D: Perceptual positions relate to the three different perspectives that we worked with in the Spiritual Healing process. 'First position' involves standing in your own shoes, feeling your own body and looking out at the world through your own eyes. 'Second position' involves putting yourself into the shoes of another person, and seeing and feeling the world from that person's perspective. 'Third position' involves taking an observer view, watching the interaction between yourself and the other person.

Creating a basic "time line" involves laying out spaces on the ground representing past, present and future. Putting these three locations for time together with the three basic perceptual positions creates a "landscape" made up of 9 locations. The landscape is essentially made up of three time lines, one for yourself, one for others and one for an observer.

1. Future Other	2. Future Self	3. Future Observer
4. Present Other	5. Present Self	6. Present Observer
7. Past Other	8. Past Self	9. Past Observer

If Robert McDonald were to stand in the middle of the grid, at location 5, he would be in "first position present." That is, he would be experiencing the "here and now" from his own perspective. (McDonald steps into location 5 - Present Self.)

M: Here, in location 5, I am seeing what I see around me in the room right now, feeling my body and hearing the sounds that are actually ongoing in this room.

D: If Robert were to step forward into location 2, he would be in "first person future." It would be as if he was walking on his time line into his future. Now, when Robert stands in location 2, he imagines that he is actually in his future - he acts "as if" he is in a future experience. For example,

let's say Robert were to step forward to our next Tools of
the Spirit seminar in Hawaii. (McDonald steps into location 2 - Future Self.)

M: As I walk here, I imagine that I'm going eight months into
the future. Standing in my future self at location 2, I
imagine that I am in Hawaii, seeing the palm trees and
beaches, hearing the waves and the Hawaiian music,
feeling the warm sunny weather, and feeling really excited about being here. And since I am now in the future,
when I look back and see myself at location 5, I experience
that Robert as being eight months in the past.

D: So, from location 2, Robert could speak to his 'present self'
in location 5 as if he were in his future looking back.
　　If Robert moved to location 1 (Future Other), he would
be stepping into the shoes of another person in the future.
For instance, he could put himself into the perspective of
one of the Tools of the Spirit participants in Hawaii.
(McDonald steps into location 1.)

M: As I stand here, I imagine being in the shoes of a person
who is at Tools of the Spirit for the first time. I see Robert
Dilts and Robert McDonald speaking to me and guiding
me. I sense the excitement of making spiritual discoveries, and feel awakened and healed as I am going through
the Sacred Journey, the Spiritual Healing process and the
other exercises.

D: If Robert moved over to location 3 (Future Observer), he
would imagine viewing this future experience as if he
were an observer. (McDonald steps into location 3.)

M: As I stand here, I feel like a wise and caring observer. I
can see Robert McDonald and the seminar participant in
Hawaii and watch them interact. I see Robert McDonald
touching the participant, and the participant is smiling at
Robert and giving him a hug.

D: It is interesting to notice that if Robert steps back into location 5 (his Present Self), he will have a much richer experience when he considers his future. (McDonald returns to location 5.)

M: My experience of my future is much clearer now. And I feel very excited and hopeful about going to Hawaii in eight months.

D: Now, in the present, Robert can also step into second and third perceptual positions. For instance, he could move to location 4 (Present Other) and put himself in my shoes, taking Robert Dilts' perspective. (McDonald steps into location 4.)

M: Here, I experience myself as if I were Robert Dilts instead of Robert McDonald. I can look over at Robert McDonald in location 5 and see his smile and sense his excitement about the program we are going to do in Hawaii eight months from now, and I like that.

D: Robert could also move over to the present observer position at location 6, and view the interaction between Robert McDonald and Robert Dilts. (McDonald steps into location 6 - Present Observer.)

M: I am able to see Robert and Robert over there, smiling at each other and touching each other. I can see that they are really committed to creating something powerful and beautiful together.

D: When Robert comes back again to first position present at location 5, his experience may be enriched even more.

M: Yes, I feel supported and guided in the present, as well as excited about the future.

D: Now if Robert stepped backwards to location 8 (Past Self), it would be as if he were walking back on a highway or a pathway leading to his past. He would become a younger Robert McDonald, maybe a Robert of 10 years ago or 20 years ago, or even further. As he put himself back in the shoes of a younger self, he would experience the Robert at location 5 (Present Self) as being in the future. (McDonald steps into location 8.)

M: Here, I am reliving what it was like when I was 13 years old. I hear my friends and family calling me "Bobby McDonald," and am seeing the house we lived in then. And I am feeling both the wonder and the insecurity of being 13.

D: If Robert now moved into location 7 (Past Other), he would put himself into the shoes of a significant other person from his past. For example, Robert could step into the shoes of his father. (McDonald steps into location 7.)

M: As I step here I become Bill McDonald. Over in location 8 (Past Self), I see my son Bobby. He's 13 years old. And as I look at 13 year old Bobby, I feel both proud and kind of sad at the same time.

D: If Robert then moved into location 9 (Past Observer), he would become a wise and caring observer of his past. He would see Bill and Bobby McDonald, and observe them interacting. (McDonald steps into location 9.)

M: Over here, I'm observing the relationship between 13 year old Bobby and his father. I can see that they care for each other, and that some healing needs to go on between them.

D: When Robert returns to first person present at location 5, he can get an even richer sense of his life "landscape." (McDonald moves to location 5 - Present Self.)

M: In addition to the excitement of the future and the support and guidance of the present, I now feel a sense of compassion about my past and a recognition of my healing mission.

Getting New Perspectives on Your Life

D: Perceiving your past and future as part of a broader landscape, as opposed to a single rigid line of time, allows you to (a) realize that there are other people's paths that intersect with yours at various times, and (b) realize that you can move experiences and resources from one part of your landscape to other locations. For example, you can bring resources and knowledge that you have in your Present Self at location 5, back to a younger you in location 8 that needed that knowledge and those resources, but did not have them yet.

M: You can also step into the shoes of a significant other in the past and imagine that you can see the future events that are to come. Let me give you an example of that. When Robert took me through this some years ago, I ran into a difficulty with my grandmother. My grandmother was a very fearful person, and I had picked up a lot of limiting beliefs from her as a boy. Even as an adult, I would sometimes experience resistances coming from those old fears and beliefs.

So Robert Dilts asked me to go back and stand in the shoes of my grandmother. As I imagined becoming her, I saw little Bobby and felt both afraid for him and critical of him. Then Robert asked me, while I was still in the shoes of my grandmother, to look ahead and see Robert McDonald at location 5, and see what Bobby would become. From my grandmother's perspective I saw myself as an adult for the first time, and felt, "Oh, you're going to become that? Wow, that's going to be amazing." There was a deep shift in my experience of my grandmother. As her, I could accept what Bobby was going to become, and support it rather than resist it. She wasn't afraid anymore and could say, "Good. Go for it!"

D: In other words, if somebody has only known you for a particular period in your life, he or she may have no knowledge of the rest of your landscape. But the fact that this person didn't see it before doesn't mean that you can't step into his or her shoes and imagine seeing the rest of the landscape from that individual's perspective. And seeing that new part of the landscape from the perspective of the other, may give you a completely different response.

Generative Change

M: The beauty of this notion of a life "landscape" is that it allows us to do more than "remedial" work. "Rebirth" is not simply fixing something from the past that has been broken.

D: "Generative" processes are about taking something that already works, taking something that is already good, and making more of it.

M: The Spiritual Renewal process allows you to take something that you like very much and spread it throughout your life. Even if you have only had a little bit of it, you can use this process to expand it and strengthen it. For example, let's say I want to have more of a sense of "spirit" or "God" in my daily life. I can bring that feeling into the Present Self location, walk up to the Future Self location and notice how it expands. When I do that, I get a sense of "Christ consciousness," of the essence of all that is merciful, good and kind. I get a sense of the generosity of the spirit becoming more and more and more. I experience what it'll be like to be in the future having this spiritual resource spread throughout my life. And then I can spread it throughout my past, and even share it with others.

Spiritual Renewal: Tending Your Garden

D: We have been preparing this landscape throughout the
Tools of the Spirit experience. In fact, our work has been
a bit like Jesus' parable of the sower and the seeds. Our
sense of "spirit" or "God" is like a seed. In the parable, the
sower throws some seeds on shallow ground. Because
there's nothing for the seeds to take root in, they never
grow. Eventually, the birds come and eat the seeds. The
purpose of the Sacred Journey and Presence of Eternity
processes were to prepare this landscape and deepen the
soil.

The next part of the parable states that some seeds fall
on rocky ground. In this case, the plants begin to spring
up, but the roots are stopped from growing deeply because
of the stones in the earth. The plants end up withering
because the roots cannot provide the appropriate strength
and nutrition. Similarly, when the roots spreading from
the seeds of the spirit are stopped by a hard place in the
heart, something is not released. The hard places need to
be removed or softened so that the plant can be appropriately anchored and the roots can reach the emotional
moisture they need. This is one of the purposes of the
Spiritual Healing process. Combining perceptual positions with the state of 'spiritual wholeness' allows us to
remove and soften the hard places in our hearts that have
arisen because of difficulties in our relationships.

According to the parable, other seeds fall among the
thorns and weeds. These are like our Shadows. The seed
sprouts, but the plant grows up side by side with the
thorns and weeds. Eventually the weed overshadows or
strangles the plant, just as we find ourselves struggling
with our Shadows. To ensure the health of the growing
plants, the gardener must remove the weeds and thorns,
and put them in their proper place. Otherwise they will
be competing for the same soil as the seeds. This is the

purpose of the Releasing Enmeshment with the Shadow and Symbolic Rebirth processes.

When the soil has been properly prepared, the seeds are able to grow freely, their roots can reach deeply into the earth, and the plant brings forth its fruits thirty, sixty or a hundredfold.

The Spiritual Renewal process involves identifying a seed that you have discovered during your Tools of the Spirit experience and planting that seed throughout the landscape of your life. This "seed" could be your awareness of your large "S" self. It could be a sense of connection with "Spirit," "God" or "Source." The Spiritual Renewal process allows you to take that seed and make more of it. For instance, you can bring that seed into your future. You can plant and nurture that seed in an important part of your past, or share it with a significant other who has been a supporter. Instead of merely holding the seed in your heart in the present, you place it in the heart of the future you, of significant others, and of a wise observer. By bringing your spiritual resource to various parts of your landscape, it is transformed and enriched.

Demonstration of the Spiritual Renewal Process

1st Position Present - Present Self

D: We are going to do a demonstration of the Spiritual Renewal process with Pat. Hello, Pat.

P: Hello.

D: Pat, can you identify some spiritual insight or experience that has come to you or returned to you as a result of your Tools of the Spirit experience? What is the spiritual "seed" that you would like to grow and nurture more of in your life landscape?

P: When I did the Self Parenting process, the gift that I got from my parents when I opened my hands was divine love. And I've really been feeling divine love from the group, from myself and from both of you, much more than I ever have in my life.

M: Wonderful.

D: In this process we'll explore some ways of making even more of that and spreading it throughout more of your life. What I'd like to ask you to do Pat, is to step into the first person present location (Present Self – location 5) and bring the experience of divine love alive in your heart, and feel as much of it as you can in your body.

M: As you feel the sense of divine love right now deep in your body, and it begins to make itself known in actual physical feelings, where in your body do you feel it? Where do you feel the sense of divine love within you?

P: In my face. It's a warmth which is spreading and radiating.

M: You feel a spreading and radiating warmth in your face.

1st Position Future - Future Self

D: In a moment, Pat, I'm going to ask you to walk forward, as if you were walking into your own future. And as you do, imagine that this sense of divine love were a seed which would continue to grow and grow, becoming more and more a part of your life. (Pat begins to walk forward slowly.)

As you go further into your future, this sense of divine love is no longer just a brief, precious moment. It seems as if you have had it for many years.

M: As you walk, you can allow your body to notice the feeling of divine love growing and intensifying.

D: It becomes more and more a part of you. Its roots grow deeply into the soil of your body and your heart, finding moisture, until you arrive at a place in your future in which your sense of divine love has become a part of your identity. Divine love is just a part of who you are naturally. (Pat stops at location 2 - Future Self.)

M: How intense is it now?

P: It's all I am.

D: Maintaining that deep sense of divine love, please turn and face the Pat who had just re-discovered this sense of divine love as a result of her Tools of the Spirit experience. (Pat turns and faces her Present Self in location 5.) As you look at her, notice that she needs a message from you. You are her future. There are insights that you have which she does not have yet. There's something that she needs to receive from you. And as you look back at this person who was just starting this journey that you've completed, what is the message that you would send her?

P: It is there, all around you. All you have to do is ask for it.

D: You would tell her, "It is there, all around you. All you have to do is ask for it." And what gesture or movement would go with those words?

P: An embrace. (Makes an embracing motion.)

D: An embrace. And what I'd like to ask you to do now is to return to this part of the landscape, taking your time, coming back along this path. (Pat walks back to location 5 - Present Self.) Now turn again to face your future. But now notice it's different from when you stood here before. There is a Pat in the future, a radiant Pat who is filled with divine love. It is all she is. And she has a message for you.

M: (McDonald stands in location 2 - Pat's Future Self) Her message is, "It is there, all around you. All you have to do is ask for it."

D: Receive her message. And notice that as you receive it, she comes forward and embraces you.

M: And she says, "It is there, all around you. All you have to do is ask for it."

D: Notice how your present experience of divine love is deepened and enriched by this message.

P: It's down in my chest now too.

D: Nice.

2nd Position Future - Future Other

M: As you look again at the future Pat, you can notice that, standing next to the radiant future Pat who is filled with divine love, is some other person who is a companion and supporter of that future Pat. It could be another person who has been with that future Pat throughout her journey to the future.

D: Perhaps it's somebody who is a mentor to her.

M: It could be a spiritual being.

D: It could be a daughter, a child, a sister, brother or mother. It could be a close friend.

M: I wonder who's in relationship with her up in this future time. Who's in relationship with Pat?

P: A friend of mine.

M: A friend of yours. Wonderful. When you're ready, I'd like you to take your experience of divine love, which has spread from your face down into your chest, and bring it as a gift to your friend in the future. (Pat slowly steps to location 1 - Future Other.)

As you step here, become that friend in the future. Bring your gift of divine love fully inside of your friend in the future. As you stand in the shoes of this other person now, notice how you are standing next to the future Pat, who is filled with divine love. And you know it because you're sharing it with her. You have been a witness to Pat's transformations. And you have been a helper and a mentor. When you're ready, you can turn and face the Pat who is just rediscovering the sense of divine love. (Pat turns and faces her Present Self in location 5)

Standing in the shoes of Pat's future friend, what message is important for you to deliver to her?

P: I always knew you could do it.

M: "I always knew you could do it." As you tell her that, allow yourself to make whatever movement is appropriate.

P: It would be another hug. (Makes an embracing motion.)

M: Another embrace. And now come back again across time and space. (Pat walks back to Present Self - location 5.)

And facing the future, you see there is the radiant future Pat, and with her is her mentor/friend. Listen to what that person says. Receive the message, "I always knew you could do it."

D: And the radiant future Pat is saying, "It's there, all you have to do is ask for it."

M: And both come and embrace you. Feel them embrace you as they whisper these things again. "I always knew you could do it."

D: "It's there. All you have to do is ask for it. It's all around you." And Pat, being fully here in first person present, what happens now with this resource?

P: I feel it all the way down to my belly now.

3rd Position Future - Future Observer

D: Notice how that seed of divine love is blossoming more and more. And holding that feeling in your body, walk up to a place in your future where you can observe you and your friend in the future. You can become a kind and wise observer who looks upon your future self and your friend with divine love. (Pat walks to location 3 - Future Observer.)

As you look through the eyes of divine love upon the future, notice the relationship between the future Pat and her friend. Perhaps you see some of the things that are blossoming or strengthening between them. See how they serve each other and help each other. And from that perspective, you can also look back and see the path Pat has taken to the future. (Pat turns and faces her Present Self at location 5.)

As you look at her path through the eyes of divine love, you can realize that she needs to receive a message from you. There is a wisdom that you have as an observer that she needs to hear. I'm wondering what would be your message for her?

P: Just open yourself to it. Pull it in. That's all you have to do.

D: What gesture goes with that message?

P: A touch on her shoulder.

D: That's nice. Now, I'd like to invite you back across this landscape to your first person present. (Pat returns to her Present Self.)

As you stand here, notice that there's a new voice coming from your future. This new voice has a very important message for you. It says, "Just open yourself to it. Pull it in. That's all you have to do."

M: At the same time, the 'future you' is saying, "It's there. It's all around you. All you have to do is ask for it."

D: And the future friend says, "I always knew you could do it."

M: Experiencing all of these messages in first position present, please notice what happens to your experience of divine love.

P: It's all the way to the floor.

2nd Position Present - Present Other

M: Allow this feeling of divine love to be fully in your body as you're standing here and now in this room. Then think of someone who is currently in your life, with whom you would like to share this resource of divine love.

P: My father.

M: Your father. Wonderful. Now imagine that your father is standing right here next to you, in the present. In a moment, you're going to take this experience of the divine love that's increasing in your body, and bring it into your father as a gift. Holding this feeling of divine love, step into your father's shoe and become him, facing the Present Pat. (Pat moves into location 4 - Present Other.)

Standing here as your father, you lovingly notice your daughter standing beside you. What message have you come all this way to give her? What is your message to your daughter?

P: I always told you that you had everything you needed. Go for it.

M: "Go for it." That's right. I wonder what movement goes with that message?

P: A hand supporting the center of her back.

M: When you're ready, allow yourself to leave the space of your father, and enter back into your body, here and now in this room in the present. (Pat returns to Present Self.)

And notice while you're standing here that your father is with you, standing to your left, supporting the center of your back, and saying to you, "I always told you that you had everything you needed. Go for it."

D: And there's also a voice from the future you saying, "Look, it's all around you. All you have to do is ask for it. It's there."

M: Your future friend is saying, "I always knew you could do it."

D: And there is a wise observer of your future telling you, "Just open to yourself. Pull it in. Open yourself. That's all you have to do."

M: Hear these voices coming to you from the future and from your father. Let them come in. Receive them. And notice how receiving them, deepens, transforms and enriches your experience of divine love.

3rd Position Present - Present Observer

D: And when you're ready, I'd like to invite you to another part of the landscape of your life. I'd like you to take your gift of divine love to a wise observer of the present. Step to your right and look through the eyes of divine love onto the relationship between Pat and her father. (Pat steps to location 6 - Present Observer.)

As an observer you can see some important things about that relationship. You can notice things about Pat and her father that even they are not aware of. Because of your wisdom and perspective, there's a message that Pat needs to receive from you.

P: It's time to move forward.

D: And is there a gesture that would go with that message?

P: Putting my arm around her.

D: And when you're ready, please come back fully associated into first position present, facing your future. (Pat returns to Present Self location.)

Hear your Present Observer as an inner voice saying, "It's time to move forward."

M: And your father says, "I always told you that you had everything you needed. Go for it."

D: The Future Observer reminds you, "Just open yourself to it. Pull it in. That's all you have to do."

M: Your future friend tells you, "I always knew you could do it."

D: And the voice of your Future Self says, "It's all around you. All you have to do is ask for it. It's there."

M: Listen as all these voices come from in front of you, and from your left and right. Receive them. Make a space for them within you. Notice how your experience of divine love enriches, blossoms and grows.

1st Position Past - Past Self

D: And then I'd like to ask you to notice that there is a space behind you, representing an important place in your past. Think of a time in your life in which having the experience of divine love would have been totally transforming. Identify an experience in which divine love is exactly the resource that you needed. You may or may not know consciously what that event is. All you need to do to find that place is to allow your heart to guide you back until you get that sense, "It's here. This is where I needed divine love the most. (Pat begins to slowly walk backwards toward location 8 - Past Self.)

M: That's right. Gently walk back slowly to the time where this divine love is needed. You'll know the time. (Pat stops at the Past Self location.)

D: Fully bring that experience of divine love back into this past self and to this past part of your landscape. Fill her heart, her body, and her face with the radiance of divine love. It is as if by some magic, something is coming to this past you from your future. Perhaps you sense some type of guidance, or the presence of a guardian angel.

M: As you stand with your body infused with divine love, you can look into the future and see a Pat who has rediscovered this divine love, and who is sharing it with you. There is a certain message that is important for her to receive from you. You're her past. You're her foundation. You're the one that made all the right decisions that allowed her to live. And now you have this resource of divine love, that you didn't have before.

D: Look at all she's going to become. She is your future. Perhaps you never knew that before. This is who you will be. And I'm wondering what message she needs to receive from you?

P: It's only going to get better and better.

D: And is there a gesture or movement that goes with the message, "It's only going to get better and better?"

P: Pointing her toward her future.

D: I'd like to invite you now to bring this message up through time to your Present Self. (Pat walks to the Present Self location.)

M: Notice that there's a voice coming from behind you saying, "It's only going to get better and better."

D: To your right, your Present Observer reminds you, "It's time to move on."

M: And the voice of your father to your left says, "I always told you that you had everything you needed. Go for it."

D: Your Future Observer calls out, "Just open yourself to it. Pull it in. That's all you have to do."

M: Your Future Friend says proudly, "I always knew you could do it."

D: And your Future Self tells you, "It's there. It's all around you. All you have to do is ask for it."

M: While standing in your first position present, receiving all these messages, how is this resource different now?

P: It's terrifically expanded throughout my entire body, going everywhere.

2nd Position Past - Past Other

D: As you stand in the light of this expanded sense of divine love, I'd like you to notice that there is another empty space behind you for a significant other in your past. Perhaps it is somebody who was an important mentor to you. Maybe it was a person in your life who wanted to be a mentor but who couldn't yet because he or she needed the resource of divine love. But if that person was able to have this greatly expanded sense of divine love that you feel now, he or she would have been able to be a helpful mentor for that past Pat. You may not know who it will be until you step back into the location of the Past Other. (Pat turns and walks to location 7 - Past Other.)

M: As you step here, you become this person from your past, bringing your gift of divine love to him or her. Divine love is exactly the resource this person would have needed to be an even better mentor, supporter or guardian to the younger Pat.

And from inside this person's experience, notice the Pat of the past. You are her mentor and supporter. From this perspective you can also see that Pat is going to grow and transform, and the divine love that you share with her is going to continue to expand into the future. Maybe you didn't know that back then. But now you can see it. I wonder what message you find important to give to the older Pat, who has rediscovered this sense of divine love as a result of her experience with Tools of the Spirit, and who is bringing it to you as a gift? What does she need to hear from you?

P: It's okay.

M: "It's okay." What movement goes with that?

P: It's a wave good-bye.

D: You can let go of that which is no longer necessary.

M: "It's okay." She needs to know that. Your message is precious to her.

D: When you're ready, return to the present Pat and receive this message from the Past Other. (Pat returns to the Present Self location.)

M: As you stand in the present, receive this important message from the Past Other. "It's okay." And notice the wave good-bye.

D: And your Past Self is saying, "It's only going to get better and better."

M: The voice of your father tells you, "I always told you that you had everything you needed. Go for it."

D: The Present Observer is saying, "It is time to move forward."

M: Your future friend says, "I always knew you could do it."

D: The Future Observer reminds you, "Just open yourself to it. Pull it in. That's all you have to do."

M: And your Future Self is calling out to you, "It's there, it's all around you. All you have to do is ask for it."

D: And as you continue to hear this chorus of voices, feel the hugs that come from the future, the supporting hand on your back, and see the wave good-bye.

M: Notice your sense of divine love and how much more there is now.

3rd Position Past - Past Observer

D: The final place we are going to plant the seed of divine love on your life landscape is that of the Past Observer. Walk back and put yourself into the position of a kind and wise observer of your past. (Pat walks to location 9 - Past Observer.)

You can look at your past through the eyes of divine love, perhaps for the first time. You're able to see a younger Pat and a significant other person with her, a person who has just now also received a gift of divine love. And perhaps you can see something in the past and in their relationship that you've never seen before. Because you can look on it now with divine love, you can see your past differently now.

M: And, as an observer, you can look forward and see all that's going to happen. Look at Pat's life and her future landscape. The Pat who has rediscovered this gift of divine love at Tools of the Spirit needs to hear from you. What is your message to her?

P: You have to let go in order to go forward.

D: "You have to let go in order to go forward." And what movement would you make?

P: Placing my hand on her heart.

D: When you're ready, take this message and come up through time to your Present Self. (Pat walks to the Present Self location.)

M: Listen very carefully to this message of great importance from your past. The wise observer is saying, "You have to let go in order to go forward," and is gently touching your heart.

D: And the significant other from your past is waving good-bye and saying, "It's okay, it's okay."

M: The wise observer of your present tells you, "It's time to move forward."

D: Your Past Self is reminding you, "It's only going to get better and better."

M: The voice of your future observer says, "Just open yourself, pull it in. That's all you have to do."

D: Your father is telling you, "I always told you that you had everything you needed. Go for it."

M: Your Future Self is letting you know, "It's there, it's all around you. All you have to do is ask for it."

D: And your future friend claims, "I always knew you could do it."

M: Keep taking in all of these messages.

D: "You have to let go in order to go forward."

M: "Just open yourself, pull it in. That's all you have to do."

D: "It's only going to get better and better."

M: "It's time to go forward."

D: "I always told you that you had everything you needed. Go for it."

M: "It's okay."

D: "It's all around you. It's there. All you have to do is ask for it."

M: Let these voices come to you now all at once like a chorus, a symphony that surrounds you and comes in big waves that swirl and merge and mix with your being.

Pat's Metaphor

D: Let these voices fill you with divine love. You have shared your gift of divine love with each of these locations around you, and it is coming back to you in these message and the touch they are sending to you. Allow your own sense of divine love to be enriched and intensified as you feel and hear and see all of the messages coming from all of the parts of the landscape of your life.

M: If all of this were to become so intense that you began to notice a metaphor or symbol that represents what you're feeling now, what would it be?

P: Old Faithful, the geyser.

D: Allow yourself to become Old Faithful, and let your body express the metaphor in a movement. Notice the variety of ways in which this geyser of divine love will continue to transform.

M: Continue to express the movements associated with your metaphor of Old Faithful. Notice how your feeling of divine love deepens in every way. Allow it to continue to spread throughout your life.

D: And isn't it nice to know that you can take something that's good and make more of it. When you give it as a gift, it comes back as a gift. Our spiritual experiences are our deepest structures, which we can transform into surface structure through our beliefs, our capabilities and our behaviors. When you bring the deep structure of 'divine love' to one part of your life landscape, it comes back as encouragement, such as the message, "Just open yourself, pull it in. That's all you have to do." When you plant it in another location, it comes back as pride - "I always knew you could do it."

M: Bringing it to another area creates motivation - "I always told you that you had everything you needed. Go for it."

D: Planting it in another brings support - "It's all around you. It's there. All you have to do is ask for it."

M: In another it brings release - "You have to let go in order to go forward."

D: The same spiritual deep structure has many different surface structures.

M: Notice this now, fully within you, spreading inside of you.

D: All of the different names for love. Pride, support, encouragement, release.

M: I wonder how this resource of divine love will continue to manifest for you tonight, tomorrow and the next day, and for the weeks, months, years and decades of your future.

D: Imagine redoing the whole process tomorrow, taking your current experience as the starting state.

P: Wow.

D: Your current experience of divine love is now a new resource. You could repeat the process, planting that as a seed in each location.

M: Wouldn't that be something!

D: This is what's called "generative" NLP. Pat could repeat the same process tomorrow with her whole body sense of divine love. She could repeat it the next day as a meditation. I believe if you did this Spiritual Renewal process everyday for two weeks, you would probably have very few problems left. Because the interesting thing about a generative process is that rather than being "problem" oriented, it is resource oriented. The problems that are ready to be solved by that resource will be spontaneously drawn to it and resolved gently and with love. You don't have to start by identifying a problem and then struggling to find a resource that you hope will produce an adequate solution.

Practicing the Spiritual Renewal Process

D: Like all of our other *Tools of the Spirit* activities, we are providing a set of instructions which can be essentially read like a script. In our *Tools of the Spirit* seminars, we usually have people do this in groups of 3. One person is the guide, whose job is to read the script. A second person is the explorer, who selects a spiritual resource and brings it to the different areas of his or her life landscape. A third person keeps track of the messages.

It can also be done in a group of 2. Once they get the basic idea, most people don't feel the need to read the script, because the process essentially involves repeating the same loop with a little variation: You walk to one of the locations, fill it with the resource, turn back to face your Present Self, send the message, return to your Present Self and receive it.

M: Really that's it. Bring the resource to a particular location, turn around, send the message, come back to your Present Self and receive it.

D: Sometimes I call this process the "Genesis Pattern." Similar to the way God reportedly created the universe, you say it, you do it, and then you see that it's good.

M: We believe that it is important to actually hear the messages. It's like a chorus of voices all around, you, coming in all at once. This has a very profound impact on your neurology. You could use the worksheets we have provided to go through this process by yourself, but we believe it's best to do this process in community.

Steps of the Spiritual Renewal Process
(Generative NLP)

1. On the floor, create nine squares of equal size, three rows and three columns, as shown below. The bottom row of squares represents the **Past**. The middle row represents the **Present**. The top row represents the **Future**. The left-hand column of squares represents **Second Position**. The middle column represents **First Position**. The right-hand column represents **Third Position**. Therefore, the middle square represents First Position Present.

2. Recall a Spiritual experience which you would like to enrich, intensify and have more fully in your life. Facing the Future, stand in <u>First Position Present</u> and fully relive the Spiritual experience — see what you saw, hear what you heard, and feel what you felt at the time of the experience. Now, touch the part of your body where you feel the Spiritual experience living.

3. While touching this part of your body, allow the Spiritual experience to increase and intensify as you slowly walk forward into <u>First Position Future</u>. Notice how bringing the Spiritual experience into this space strengthens and enriches the experience. Now, face the "you" standing in <u>First Position Present</u>, and offer a message to him or her that reflects your deeper understanding of what is needed.

Message from 1st Position Future - **Future Self**:

4. Now, physically return to <u>First Position Present</u>, face the you in <u>First Position Future</u> and receive the message from your future self. Notice and declare how this message even further enriches your experience of Spirit.

5. Now, think of someone who will be with you in that future. And while touching the part of your body where your Spiritual experience lives, slowly walk forward into <u>Second Position Future</u>, and become the person who will be with you in the future. Now, face the you who is still standing in <u>First Position Present</u>, and offer a message to him or her that reflects your deeper understanding of what is needed.

Message from 2nd Position Future - **Future Other**:

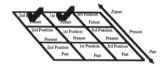

6. Now, physically return to <u>First Position Present</u>, face the you in <u>Second Position Future</u> and receive the message from your future companion. Notice and declare how this message even further enriches your experience of Spirit.

7. Now, think of what it is like to be a kind and wise observer. And while touching the part of your body where your Spiritual experience lives, slowly walk forward into <u>Third Position Future</u>. Become a kind observer of the relationship between those people standing in <u>First Position Future</u> (yourself) and <u>Second Position Future</u> (the other person). Now, face the you who is still standing in <u>First Position Present</u>, and offer a

message to him or her that reflects your deeper understanding of what is needed.

Message from 3rd Position Future - **Future Observer**:

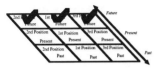

---

8. Now, physically return to <u>First Position Present</u>, face the you in <u>Third Position Future</u> and receive the message from the kind future observer. Notice and declare how the message even further enriches your experience of Spirit.

9. Now, think of someone who shares your life at present. And while touching the part of your body where your Spiritual experience lives, slowly step into <u>Second Position Present</u>, and become the person who shares your present life. Now, face the you who is still standing in <u>First Position Present</u>, and offer a message to him or her that reflects your deeper understanding of what is needed.

Message from 2nd Position Present - **Present Other**:

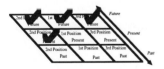

---

10. Now, physically return to <u>First Position Present</u>, face the you in <u>Second Position Present</u> and receive the message from your current companion. Notice and

declare how the message even further enriches your experience of Spirit.

11. Now, again think of what it is like to be a kind and wise observer. And while touching the part of your body where your Spiritual experience lives, slowly step into Third Position Present. Become a kind observer of the relationship between those people standing in First Position Present (yourself) and Second Position Present (the other person). Now, face the you who is still standing in First Position Present, and offer a message to him or her that reflects your deeper understanding of what is needed.

Message from 3rd Position Present - **Present Observer**:

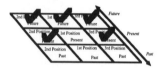

---

12. Now, physically return to First Position Present, face the you in Third Position Present and receive the message from the kind observer. Notice and declare how the message even further enriches your experience of Spirit.

13. Now, think of a time in your past when this Spiritual experience would have helped you in some way. And while touching the part of your body where your spiritual experience lives, slowly walk backward into First Position Past, until you become the younger you. Now, face the you who is still standing in First Position Present, and offer a message to him or her that reflects your deeper understanding of what is needed.

Message from 1st Position Past - **Past Self**:

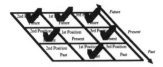

---

14. Now, physically return to <u>First Position Present</u>, face the you in <u>First Position Past</u> and receive the message from your younger self. Notice and declare how the message even further enriches your experience of Spirit.

15. Now, think of someone who shared your life in that past time. And while touching the part of your body where your Spiritual experience lives, slowly walk backward into <u>Second Position Past</u>, and become the person who shared your earlier life. Now, face the you who is still standing in <u>First Position Present</u>, and offer a message to him or her that reflects your deeper understanding of what is needed.

Message from 2nd Position Past - **Past Other**:

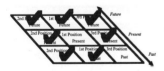

---

16. Now, physically return to <u>First Position Present</u>, face the you in <u>Second Position Past</u> and receive the message from your young companion. Notice and declare how the message even further enriches your experience of Spirit.

17. Now, again think of what it is like to be a kind observer. And while touching the part of your body where your Spiritual experience lives, slowly walk backward into <u>Third Position Past</u>. Become a kind observer of the relationship between those people standing in <u>First Position Past</u> (yourself) and <u>Second Position Past</u> (the other person). Also, kindly observe your entire life, spread out from the Past, through the Present and into the Future. Now, face the you who is still standing in <u>First Position Present</u>, and offer a message to him or her that reflects your deeper understanding of what is needed.

Message from 3rd Position Past - **Past Observer**:

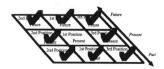

18. Now, physically return to <u>First Position Present</u>, face the you in <u>Third Position Past</u> and receive the message from the kind observer. Notice and declare how the message even further enriches your experience of Spirit.

19. Now, while standing in <u>First Position Present</u>, listen to each message coming to you from each of the locations. And then listen to all the messages combine into a chorus of voices gracefully surrounding you and becoming a single sound.

20. As you listen to the single sound and feel the intensity of the Spiritual experience in every part of your body, allow a metaphor to emerge that represents what you are feeling. Then become the metaphor and allow your body to express the metaphor in movement. And now, notice a variety of ways in which this Spiritual Renewal will continue to spread throughout your life.

Chapter 11

Closing

Overview of Chapter 11

- **Final Drawings of the Large "S" Self**
- **Readings**
- **Is the Universe a Friendly Place?**

Final Drawings of the Large "S" Self

D: At the end of our *Tools of the Spirit* courses, we ask participants to make a final drawing of themselves, incorporating any spiritual transformations they may have experienced. We recommend that you do this now, as a way to anchor and reaccess your Tools of the Spirit experience. You may use the space provided below.

Readings

M: Another part of our closing ritual is to read some poems or sayings which we find to be inspiring "tools of the spirit." One of my favorites is from Symeon The New Theologian, who lived more than 1000 years ago. He said something which was probably considered quite blasphemous at the time, but which makes sense to my spirit. He wrote:

> *We awaken in Christ's body*
> *as Christ awakens our bodies,*
> *and my poor hand is Christ, He enters*
> *my foot, and is infinitely me.*
>
> *I move my hand, and wonderfully*
> *my hand becomes Christ, becomes all of Him*
> *(for God is indivisibly*
> *whole, seamless in His Godhood).*
>
> *I move my foot, and at once*
> *He appears like a flash of lightning.*
> *Do my words seem blasphemous?—Then*
> *open your heart to Him*
>
> *and let yourself receive the one*
> *who is opening to you so deeply.*
> *For if we genuinely love Him,*
> *we wake up inside Christ's body*
>
> *where all our body, all over,*
> *every most hidden part of it,*
> *is realized in joy as Him,*
> *and He makes us, utterly real,*
>
> *and everything that is hurt, everything*
> *that seemed to us dark, harsh, shameful,*
> *maimed, ugly, irreparably*
> *damaged, is in Him transformed*

and recognized as whole, as lovely,
and radiant in His light
we awaken as the Beloved
in every last part of our body.

D: Remember, you don't have to hear the term "Christ" only in relation to the traditional Christian perspective. You could understand "Christ" to mean "God" or "Spirit", or whatever is most appropriate for you.

M: For me, "Christ" means anything that touches me as merciful, healing and transforming.

D: One of my favorites is a poem by e.e. cummings. To me, it represents rebirth. He wrote:

i thank You God for most this amazing day:
for the leaping greenly spirits of trees
and a blue true dream of sky;
and for everything which is natural which is
infinite
which is yes
(i who have died am alive again today,
and this is the sun's birthday;
this is the birth day of life and of love and wings;
and of the gay great happening illimitably earth)

how should tasting touching hearing seeing
breathing any — lifted from the no of all nothing —
human merely being
doubt unimaginable You?

(now the ears of my ears awake and
now the eyes of my eyes are opened)

Is the Universe a Friendly Place?

D: I consider Albert Einstein to be one of my spiritual mentors and teachers. I was born in the same hospital in which Albert Einstein was dying in Princeton, New Jersey. I was born at the same time he was dying. So I was coming and he was going.

There is an interesting anecdote about a reporter who was interviewing Einstein toward the end of his life. The reporter asked, "Dr. Einstein, you're considered to be a great genius. In fact, you're often considered to be the symbol for genius in our century. Your thoughts have spanned everything from the atom to the cosmos. You're considered to be both a great scientist and also a great humanitarian and thinker. You are known to be a pacifist, and yet at the same time your discoveries and ideas have been used to create some of the most horrible weapons for destruction in existence. Given this frame, what do you think is the most important question facing humanity?" Before answering, Einstein characteristically looked up and right, into space for a moment, and then he looked down at the ground in front of him. Finally, he looked back at the reporter and said, "I think that the most important question facing humanity is, 'Is the universe a friendly place?' Because if we decide that the universe is inherently unfriendly, then we're going to use our knowledge and our technology to create greater weapons and bigger walls with which to destroy or shut out the unfriendliness. And I believe we're getting to a point where our weapons can destroy ourselves. If we decide that the universe is neither friendly nor unfriendly, and that God is playing dice with the universe, then nothing matters. What you do doesn't really have meaning, it's just a matter of the throw of the dice. If, on the other hand, we decide that the universe is a friendly place, then power and safety, rather than coming through weapons and walls, will come through using our knowledge and our technologies to create tools to better understand the universe and its positive purposes. With such tools we can identify and direct the friendliness."

I think that says something about "Tools of the Spirit." Incidentally, to say that it's a "friendly universe" doesn't mean that it's inherently safe. If we have the tools to find positive purposes, however, we can create a context of safety in which we can grow and thrive.

You might wonder, "If people have positive intentions, why do they do such bad things? Why do people behave in an evil manner if they have positive purposes?" According to our understanding of Tools of the Spirit, if you have a positive intention but a very limited map of the world, then that map constricts the ways in which you can achieve and express your positive intention. If your map of the world is founded on fear and violence, then whether you're trying to protect somebody or trying to have fun, you're going to do it through a filter of fear and violence. This is why the mission of Tools of the Spirit is to create more methods to widen our maps of the world.

It has been suggested that, rather than think of ourselves as human beings having a spiritual experience, we are spiritual beings having a human experience. An especially powerful quote for me, which expresses this view, is one from Albert Einstein, who said:

"A human being is a part of the whole called by us 'universe'...a part limited in time and space. He experiences his thoughts and feelings as separated from the rest — a kind of optical delusion of his consciousness. This delusion is a kind of prison for us, restricting us to our personal desires and to affection for a few persons nearest us. Our task must be to free ourselves from this prison by widening our circle of compassion to embrace all living creatures and the whole of nature in its beauty."

Appendix A:
Some Tools of the Spirit;
Quotations, Songs and Readings

D: Appendix A provides a collection of some readings, songs, poems and quotations that we have found to be personally inspiring. Our intention with this section is to share some of our own personal "spiritual tools" - writings that we found to be useful for putting us more in touch with our larger "S" selves. We hope that they offer some examples of different types of 'tools of the spirit'.

As part of this collection, for instance, we have summarized some of the fundamental presuppositions of NLP, and included more in depth definitions of key spiritual concepts and models.

M: I created an 'emotional and spiritual vocabulary' which presents our working definitions for many of the key words we have referred to in this book. There is also an excellent article, *On Defining the Spirit*, by Rachel Naomi Remen, which gives some ideas about what "spirit" is, and is not.

D: There's a quotation from David Bohm, and a summary of what Aldous Huxley called "the perennial philosophy" by Ken Wilber, which has to do with recurring themes in spiritual experiences and literature. We have also included various quotations which we think are quite relevant to many of the themes we have presented. They emphasize different dimensions of what we have covered in this book.

M: In the section entitled Embracing the Vision of NLP, there are some valuable quotations by Thich Nhat Hahn, Rumi, Mother Teresa, Meister Eckart, Carlos Castenada and

Albert Einstein among others. There are also poems by e.e. cummings, Symeon the New Theologian, and a description of 'faith'.

D: The last quotation is drawn from the opening lines of Genesis. To me this represents the generative aspects of spirit. It's not intended as a scientific or nonscientific statement. I've always found it to be very moving. For me, it represents the essential nature of "God" as creative rather than punitive.

M: Frequently, prior to doing a "Tools of the Spirit" seminar, Robert and I will review some of these readings to prepare ourselves spiritually.

D: Remember that the map is not the territory. These various readings and quotations are a personal collection made by Robert and me, and are not intended to be a "hymnal" or "sacred text." Rather, they are examples of definitions, poems, quotations and songs that we have collected together which represent various aspects of 'spirit' for us. We invite you to read them at your leisure. If you don't like them, put them aside. If they strike a chord with you, then feel free to meditate on them. Above all, enjoy them.

We hope these quotations will inspire you to collect some of your own "tools of the spirit."

Presuppositions of NLP

The Map is not the Territory.

1. People respond to their own perceptions of reality.

2. Every person has their own individual map of the world. No individual map of the world is any more "real" or "true" than any other.

3. The meaning of a communication to another person is the response it elicits in that person, regardless of the intent of the communicator.

4. The 'wisest' and most 'compassionate' maps are those which make available the widest and richest number of choices, as opposed to being the most "real" or "accurate".

5. People already have (or potentially have) all of the resources they need to act effectively.

6. People make the best choices available to them given the possibilities and the capabilities that they perceive available to them from their model of the world. Any behavior no matter how evil, crazy or bizarre it seems is the best choice available to the person at that point in time - if given a more appropriate choice (within the context of their model of the world) the person will be more likely to take it.

7. Change comes from releasing the appropriate resource, or activating the potential resource, for a particular context by enriching a person's map of the world.

Life And 'Mind' Are Systemic Processes.

1. The processes that take place within a person, and between people and their environment, are systemic. Our bodies, our societies and our universe form an ecology of systems and sub-systems all of which interact with, and mutually influence, each other.

2. It is not possible to completely isolate any part of a system from the rest of the system. People cannot not influence each other. Interactions between people form feedback loops - such that a person will be effected by the results that their own actions make on other people.

3. Systems are 'self organizing' and naturally seek states of balance and stability. There are no failures, only feedback.

4. No response, experience or behavior is meaningful outside of the context in which it was established or the response it elicits next. Any behavior, experience or response may serve as a resource or limitation depending on how it fits in with the rest of the system.

5. Not all interactions in a system are on the same level. What is positive on one level may be negative on another level. It is useful to separate behavior from "self" - to separate the positive intent, function, belief, etc. that generates the behavior from the behavior itself.

6. At some level all behavior is (or at one time was) "positively intended". It is or was perceived as appropriate given the context in which it was established, from the point of view of the person whose behavior it is. It is easier and more productive to respond to the intention rather than the expression of a problematic behavior.

7. Environments and contexts change. The same action will not always produce the same result. In order to successfully adapt and survive, a member of a system needs a certain minimum amount of flexibility. That amount of flexibility has to be proportional to the variation in the rest of the system. As a system becomes more complex, more flexibility is required.

8. If what you are doing is not getting the response you want, then keep varying your behavior until you do elicit the response.

An Emotional and Spiritual Vocabulary

Birth: Entering duality, the profane.

Suffering: Experiences which arise when we are separate from God: change, impermanence and death; multiple disassociations from pain.

Pain: The natural discomfort of living in duality.

Hurt: Meaningless pain.

Fear: Anticipating future hurt.

Sin: Loveless perception

Authenticity: Congruence of body, emotions, mind and spirit.

Humility: Surrendering to personal boundaries and limitations, to that which cannot be controlled.

Gratitude: Authentic thanksgiving for this life as it is.

Ritual: A grateful celebration of our ultimate belonging.

Mercy: Breaking rules in service of the heart.

Forgiveness: Giving as you gave before the hurt occurred.

Grace: Unmerited mercy.

Truth: That which is as it is.

Death: Letting go of the unnecessary.

Rebirth: Awakening to universal innocence, the sacred.

Faith: Consciously participating in universal innocence.

Love: Fully participating in the face of change, impermanence and death.

Spiritual Healing: A rebirth of loving the truth of the mundane.

God: The Mystery to which we ultimately belong, and which ultimately belongs to us, like the air.

Spiritual: The "experience" of ultimate belonging, the fragrance of God, like the wind or breath.

Spiritual Practice: A dedicated activity which reminds us of our ultimate belonging and restores loving perception.

Awareness: The ineffable, indescribable state of consciousness behind the structure of thought.

Ministry: Any interaction which results in an expanded awareness of universal innocence.

Therapy: Any interaction which results in an expanded awareness of personal innocence.

Education: Any interaction which results in additional skills.

NLP: A Meta-Tool which studies "thought," the structure of duality; it creates Tools of the Spirit.

Tools Of The Spirit: Aids which lead us to Awareness, the gateway to God.

On Defining the Spirit

What then is the spiritual? I find it difficult to define directly. It's much easier to say what it isn't than what it is.

For example—the spiritual is often confused with the moral, but it's not the moral. Morality is concerned with issues of right and wrong. Although often attributed to the "godhead," it actually has a social basis and reflects a social tradition or consensus. What is considered moral varies from culture to culture and from time to time within the same culture. Furthermore, morality often serves as the basis for judgment, for one group of people separating themselves from other groups, or one individual separating from others. Yet the spiritual is profoundly non-judgmental and non-separative. The spiritual does not vary from time to time because it is not within time. Spirit is unchanging.

The spiritual is also different from the ethical. Ethics is a set of values, a code for translating the moral into daily life. It defines the right way to relate to other people, to carry out business and to behave in general. If the moral is not the spiritual, then the ethical isn't either.

The spiritual is also not the psychic. The psychic is a capacity we all share, although it is better developed in some people than in others. It is a way of perceiving—a sort of direct knowing of conditions in matter or in consciousness. We may use a psychic power to know the spiritual—but that which we know is not the means by which we know. As a way of perception, the psychic is closely related to our other senses. If psychic perception is spiritual—then seeing is spiritual and hearing is spiritual. A sense is simply a way of gaining information about the world around us. How I use what I see or hear, what it means to me, is what makes it a matter of spirit or not. I can use the psychic as I can use my other senses—to impress others, to accumulate personal power, to dominate or manipulate—in short to assert my separateness and my personal power. The spiritual however is not separative. A deep sense of the spiritual leads one to trust not one's own lonely power but the great flow or pattern manifested in all life, including our own. We become not manipulator but witness.

Oddly, the psychic is often used to "prove" the spiritual to the non-believer. Yet the spiritual is the one dimension of human experience which does not require proof—which lies beyond (and includes) the very mind which demands proof.

Lastly, the spiritual is not the religious. A religion is a dogma, a set of beliefs about the spiritual and a set of practices which arise out of those beliefs. There are many religions and they tend to be mutually exclusive. That is, every religion tends to think that it has "dibs" on the spiritual—that it's "The Way." Yet the spiritual is inclusive. It is the deepest sense of belonging and participation. We all participate in the spiritual at all times, whether we know it or not. There's no place to go to be separated from the spiritual, so perhaps one might say that the spiritual is that realm of human experience which religion attempts to connect us to through dogma and practice. Sometimes it succeeds and sometimes it fails. Religion is a bridge to the spiritual. Unfortunately in seeking the spiritual we may become attached to the bridge rather than crossing over it.

The most important thing in defining spirit is the recognition that spirit is an essential need of human nature. There is something in all of us that seeks the spiritual. This yearning varies in strength from person to person but it is always there in everyone. And so, healing becomes possible. Yet there is a culture-wide tendency to deny the spiritual—to delegate it at best, to ignore it at worst. In trying to point to it with a definition, I hope to initiate a kind of questioning of the role of spirit in health, in health care and in life.

– Rachel Naomi Remen (The Noetic Journal)

The Finite and The Infinite

In considering the relationship between the finite and the infinite, we are led to observe that the whole field of the finite is inherently limited, in that it has no independent existence . . . . We can see this dependent nature of the finite from the fact that every finite thing is transient . . . .

But if the finite has no independent existence, it cannot be all that is. We are thus led to propose that the true ground of all being is the infinite, the unlimited; and that the infinite includes and contains the finite . . . .

The field of the finite is all that we can see, hear, touch, remember, and describe . . . . The essential quality of the infinite, by contrast, is its subtlety, its intangibility. This quality is conveyed in the word *spirit*, whose root meaning is *wind*, or *breath*. This suggests an invisible but pervasive energy, to which the manifest world of the finite responds. This energy, or spirit, infuses all living beings, and without it any organism must fall apart into its constituent elements. That which is truly alive in the living being is this energy or spirit, and this is never born and never dies.

David Bohm
(1917 - 1992)

Summary of The Perennial Philosophy

The <u>Perennial Philosophy</u> as described in **Grace and Grit** (1991) by Ken Wilber.

1. *Spirit exists*

2. *Spirit is found within.*

3. *We are living in a world of sin, separation and duality; a fallen or illusory state. Most of us don't therefore realize this Spirit within.*

4. *There is a way out of this fallen state of sin, illusion and duality: a pathway to liberation.*

5. *The Path will take us to Rebirth or Enlightenment, i.e., a direct experience of Spirit within, a Supreme Liberation.*

6. *Direct experience of Spirit within marks the end of sin and suffering.*

7. *This results in social actions of mercy and compassion on behalf of all sentient beings.*

"Just as the human body universally grows hair and the human mind universally grows ideas, so the human spirit universally grows intuitions of the Divine. And those intuitions and insights form the core of the world's great spiritual or wisdom traditions. And again, although the surface structures of the great traditions are most certainly quite different, their deep structures are quite similar, often identical. Thus, it's mostly the deep structures of the human encounter of the Divine that the perennial philosophy is interested in."

1. "Spirit exists, God exists, a Supreme Reality exists. Brahman Dharmakaya, Kether, Tao, Allah, Shiva, Yahweh, Aton — 'They call Him many who is really One.'"

2. "Spirit is within, there is a universe within. The stunning
   message of the mystics is that in the very core of your
   being, you are God. Strictly speaking, God is neither
   within nor without — Spirit transcends all duality. But
   one discovers this by consistently looking within, until
   'within' becomes 'beyond.'" . . . . . "In fact, the individual
   self or ego is precisely what blocks the realization of the
   Supreme Identity in the first place. Rather, the 'you' in
   question is the deepest part of you—or, if you wish, the
   highest part of you— the subtle essence, as the Upanishad
   put it, that transcends your mortal ego and directly
   partakes of the Divine."

3. ". . . I cannot perceive my own true identity, or my union
   with Spirit, because my awareness is clouded and ob-
   structed by a certain activity that I am now engaged in.
   And that activity, although known by many different
   names, is simply the activity of contracting and focusing
   awareness on my individual self or personal ego. My
   awareness is not open, relaxed, and God-centered, it is
   closed, contracted, and self-centered. And precisely because I am identified with the self-contraction to the
   exclusion of everything else, I can't find or discover my
   prior identity, my true identity, with the All. My individual nature, 'the natural man,' is thus fallen, or lives in
   sin and separation and alienation from Spirit and from
   the rest of the world."
   . . . . "And according to the perennial philosophy,
   awareness dominated by the self-contraction, by the sub-
   ject/object dualism, cannot perceive reality as it is, reality
   in its wholeness, reality as the Supreme Identity. Sin, in
   other words, is the self-contraction, the separate-self
   sense, the ego. Sin is not something the self does, it is
   something the self is." . . . . "'Sin,' 'suffering,' and 'self' are

so many names for the same process, the same contraction or fragmentation of awareness. You cannot rescue the self from suffering. As Gautama Buddha put it, to end suffering you must end the self — they rise and fall together."

. . . . . "This 'small self' or individual soul is known in Sanskrit as the ahamkara which means 'knot' or 'contraction,' and it is this ahamkara, this dualistic or egocentric contraction in awareness, that is at the root of our fallen state."

4. ". . . There is a way to reverse the Fall, a way to reverse this brutal state of affairs, a way to untie the knot of illusion." . . . . "If we want to discover our identity with the All, then our case of mistaken identity with the isolated ego must be let go. Now this Fall can be reversed instantly by understanding that in reality it never actually happened—there is only God, the separate self is an illusion. But for most of us, the Fall has to be reversed gradually, step by step." . . . . "In other words, the fourth point of the perennial philosophy is that a Path exists—a Path that, if followed properly, with lead us from our fallen state to our enlightened state, from samasara to nirvana, from Hell to Heaven." . . . .

". . . Swami Ramdas, 'There are two ways: one is to expand your ego to infinity, and the other is to reduce it to nothing, the former by knowledge, and the latter by devotion. The Jnani (knowledge holder) says: "I am God—the Universal Truth." The devotee says: "I am nothing, O God, You are everything." In both cases, the ego-sense disappears.'"

5. ". . . a Rebirth, Resurrection, or Enlightenment. In your own being, the small self must die so that the big Self may resurrect." . . . . "This process of turning from 'manhood'

to 'Godhood,' or from outer person to inner person, or from self to the Self, is known in Christianity as metanoia, which means both 'repentance' and 'transformation'—we repent of the self (or sin) and transform the Self (or Christ), so that, as you said, 'not I but Christ liveth in me.'" . . . "This 'turning about' is simply the undoing of the habitual tendency to create a separate and substantial self where there is in fact only vast, open, clear awareness. This turning about or metanoia, Zen calls satori or kenshno. 'Ken' means true nature and 'sho' means 'directly seeing.' Directly seeing one's true nature is becoming Buddha." (Enlightenment is): "Actual ego-death, yes. It's no metaphor." ". . . . all of a sudden you simply wake up and discover that, among other things, your real being is everything you are now looking at, that you are literally one with all manifestation, one with the universe, however corny that might sound, and that you did not actually become one with God and All, you have eternally been that oneness but didn't realize it." "Along with this feeling . . . . goes the very concrete feeling that your small self simply died, actually died." Eckhart: "The kingdom of God is for none but the thoroughly dead."

"The Self doesn't live forever in time, it lives in the timeless present prior to time, prior to history, change, succession. The Self is present as Pure Presence, not as everlasting duration, a rather horrible notion."

6. ". . . enlightenment or liberation brings an end to suffering. Gautama Buddha . . . said that he only taught two things, what causes suffering and how to end it. What causes suffering is the grasping and desiring of the separate self, and what ends it is the meditative path that transcends self and desire. The point is that suffering is inherent in the knot or contraction known as self, and the only way to end suffering is to end the self. It's not that

after enlightenment, or after spiritual practice in general, you no longer feel pain or anguish or fear or hurt. You do. It's simply that they no longer threaten your existence, and so they cease to be problematic. You are no longer identified with them, dramatizing them, energizing them, threatened by them." "Suffering comes and goes,but the person now possesses the 'peace that surpasseth understanding.' The sage feels suffering, but it doesn't 'hurt.' Because the sage is aware of suffering, he or she is motivated by compassion, by a desire to help all those who suffer and think it's real."

7. "True enlightenment is said to issue in social action driven by mercy, compassion, and skillful means, in an attempt to help all beings attain the supreme liberation. Enlightened activity is simply selfless service. Since we are all one in the same Self, or the same mystical body of Christ . . . then in serving others I am serving my own Self."

Embracing the Vision of NLP

"All healing is essentially the release from fear." **A Course in Miracles**

"So what did you think it was that needed to be loved? **Thaddeus Golas**

"The real miracle is not to walk either on water or on thin air, but to walk on earth." **Thich Nhat Hahn**

"When we can't protect ourselves anymore, only mercy remains." **Stephen Levine**

"Through love, all pain will turn to medicine." **Rumi**

"I don't know what your destiny will be, but one thing I do know: the only ones among you who will be really happy are those who have sought and found how to serve." **Albert Schweitzer**

"Complete possession is proved only by giving. All you are unable to give possesses you." **Andre Gide**

"Deep within abides another life, not like the life of the senses, escaping sight, unchanging. This endures when all created things have passed away." **Hinduism**

"A human being is an opportunity for the infinite to manifest." **Angeles Arrien**

"The only way to learn compassion is through our own broken hearts, we have to back up and pass through our own pain." **Matthew Fox**

"I keep my ideals, because in spite of everything I still believe that people are really good at heart." **Anne Frank**

"Seldom, or perhaps never, does a marriage develop into an individual relationship smoothly and without crises; there is no coming into consciousness without pain." **Carl Jung**

"My religion is very simple. My religion is kindness." **The Dalai Lama**

"What is obvious to me is that we did not create ourselves . . . life is something in side of you. You did not create it. Once you understand that, you are in a spiritual realm." **Virginia Satir**

"I am sure that if we all understand The Golden Rule — that God is Love and that He has created us for greater things, to love and to be loved — we would then love one another as He has loved each one of us. True love is giving until it hurts. It is not how much we give — but how much we put into the giving. Therefore it is necessary to pray — the fruit of prayer is the deepening of Faith — the fruit of Faith is Love — Love in action is Service — and so acts of Love are acts of Peace — and this is the living of The Golden Rule. Love one another as God loves each one of us. God Bless You." **Mother Teresa**

"Let nothing disturb you. Let nothing frighten you. Everything passes away except God." **Saint Theresa**

"Sometimes I go about pitying myself, and all the time I am being carried on great winds across the sky." **Ojibway**

"We who lived in concentration camps can remember the men who walked through the huts comforting others, giving away their last piece of bread. They may have been few in number, but they offer sufficient proof that everything can be taken away from a man but one thing: the last of the human freedoms—to choose one's attitude in any given set of circumstances, to choose one's own way." **Viktor Frankl**

"If the only prayer you say in your whole life is 'thank you,' that would suffice." **Meister Eckhart**

"[K]nowledge of what is does not open the door directly to what should be. One can have the clearest and most complete knowledge of what is, and yet not be able to deduct from that what should be the goal of our human aspirations...[O]ur existence and our activity acquire meaning only by the setting up of such a goal and of corresponding values."
"Perfection of means and confusion of goals seem - in my opinion - to characterize our age."
"[T]he ancients knew something which we seem to have forgotten. All means prove but a blunt instrument, if they have not behind them a living spirit. But if the longing for the achievement of the goal is powerfully alive within us, then we shall not lack the strength to find the means for reaching the goal and for translating it into deeds."
"If we desire sincerely and passionately the safety, the welfare and the free development of the talents of all men, we shall not be in want of the means to approach such a state. Even if only a small part of mankind strives for such goals, their superiority will prove itself in the long run." - **Albert Einstein**

"...any ongoing ensemble of events and objects which has the appropriate complexity of causal circuits and the appropriate energy relations will surely show mental characteristics.
"...no part of such an internally interactive system can have unilateral control over any other part. The mental characteristics are inherent or immanent in the ensemble as a whole..

"The individual mind is immanent but not only in the body. It is immanent in pathways and messages outside the body; and there is a larger Mind of which the individual mind is only a sub-system. This larger Mind is comparable to God and is perhaps what people mean by "God", but it is still immanent in the total interconnected social system and planetary ecology." - **Gregory Bateson**

All Bibles or sacred codes have been the causes of the following errors: One, that man has two real existing principles, viz, a body and a soul. Two that energy, called 'evil', is alone from the body, and that reason, called good, is alone from the soul. Three, that God will torment man in eternity for following his energies.
But the following contraries are true: One, that man has no body distinct from his soul. For that which is called body is a portion of soul discerned by the five senses, the chief inlets of soul in this age. Two, energy is the only life and is from the body, and reason is the outward bound or circumference of energy. Three, energy is eternal delight. - **William Blake**

...we are luminous beings. We are perceivers. We are an awareness; we are not objects; we have no solidity. We are boundless. The world of objects and solidity is a way of making our passage on earth convenient. It is only a description that was created to help us. We forget that the description is only a description and thus we entrap the totality of ourselves in a vicious circle from which we rarely emerge in our lifetime.
The question is not whether [the warrior] will make decisions but whether he will choose impeccably from a wide variety of possible responses to the given situation. - **Carlos Castaneda**

Matter possesses gravity in virtue of its tendency toward a central point. It is essentially composite; consisting of parts that exclude each other. It seeks Unity; and therefore exhib-

its itself as self-destructive, as verging toward its opposite
[an indivisible point]. If it could attain this it would be
matter no longer, it would have perished. Spirit, on the
contrary, may be defined as that which has its center in
itself. It has not a unity outside itself, but has already found
it; it exists in and within itself. Matter has its essence out of
itself; Spirit is self-contained existence. Now this is Freedom
exactly. For if I am dependent, my being is referred something else which I am not; I cannot exist independently of
something external. I am free on the contrary when my
existence depends upon myself.

The final cause of the world at large, we allege to be the
consciousness of its own freedom on the part of Spirit, and
ipso facto, the reality of that freedom. **- Georg Hegel**

AMAZING GRACE

Amazing Grace, how sweet the sound
That saved a wretch like me
I once was lost but now I'm found
Was blind but now I see

'Twas Grace that taught my heart to fear
And Grace my fears relieved
How precious did that Grace appear
The hour I first believed

Through many dangers, toils and snares
I have already come
'Tis Grace that brought me safe thus far
And Grace will lead me home

When we've been there ten thousand years
Bright shining as the sun
We've no less days to sing God's praise
Than when we first begun.

Amazing Grace, how sweet the sound
That saved a wretch like me
I once was lost but now I'm found
Was blind but now I see

<u>Readings</u>

i thank You God for most this amazing day:
for the leaping greenly spirits of trees
and a blue true dream of sky;
and for everything which is natural which is
infinite
which is yes
(i who have died am alive again today,
and this is the sun's birthday;
this is the birth day of life and of love and wings;
and of the gay great happening illimitably earth)

how should tasting touching hearing seeing
breathing any — lifted from the no of all nothing
—
human merely being
doubt unimaginable You?

(now the ears of my ears awake and
now the eyes of my eyes are opened)

e. e. cummings

We awaken in Christ's body
as Christ awakens our bodies,
and my poor hand is Christ, He enters
my foot, and is infinitely me.

I move my hand, and wonderfully
my hand becomes Christ, becomes all of Him
(for God is indivisibly
whole, seamless in His Godhood).

I move my foot, and at once
He appears like a flash of lightning.
Do my words seem blasphemous?—Then
open your heart to Him

and let yourself receive the one
who is opening to you so deeply.
For if we genuinely love Him,
we wake up inside Christ's body

where all our body, all over,
every most hidden part of it,
is realized in joy as Him,
and He makes us, utterly real,

and everything that is hurt, everything
that seemed to us dark, harsh, shameful,
maimed, ugly, irreparably
damaged, is in Him transformed

and recognized as whole, as lovely,
and radiant in His light
we awaken as the Beloved
in every last part of our body.

Symeon The New Theologian (949-1022)

If anyone asks you
how the perfect satisfaction
of all our sexual wanting
will look, lift your face and say,
　like this.

When someone mentions the gracefulness
of the night sky, climb up on the roof
and dance and say,
　like this?

If anyone wants to know what "spirit" is,
or what "God's fragrance" means,
lean your head toward him or her,
keep your face there close.
　Like this.

When someone quotes the old poetic image
about clouds gradually uncovering the moon,
slowly loosen knot by knot the strings
of your robe.
　Like this?

If anyone wonders how Jesus raised the dead,
don't try to explain the miracle.
Kiss me on the lips.
　Like this. Like this.

When someone asks what it means
to "die for love," point
　here.

When someone asks what there is to do,
light the candle in his hand.
　Like this.

Rumi

Faith

When we walk to the edge of all the
light we have
And take that step into the darkness
of the unknown,
We must believe that one of two
things will happen:
There will be something solid for us to
stand on,
or we will be taught
how to fly.

Patrick Overtor

*In the beginning God created the heaven and the Earth.
And the Earth was without form and void; and darkness
was upon the face of the deep. And the spirit of God
moved upon the face of the waters. And God said, Let
there be light: and there was light.And God saw the light,
that it was good: and God divided the light from the
darkness. And God called the light Day, and the
darkness he called Night. And the evening and the
morning were the first day.*

*And God said, Let there be a firmament in the midst of
the waters, and let it divide the waters from the waters.
And God made the firmament, and divided the waters
which were under the firmament from the waters which
were above the firmament: and it was so. And God called
the firmament Heaven. And the evening and morning
were the second day.*

*And God said, Let the waters under the heaven be
gathered together unto one place, and let the dry land
appear: and was so. And God called the dry land Earth;
and the waters called he the Seas: and God saw that it
was good...And the earth brought forth grass, and herb
yielding seed after his kind, and the tree yielding fruit,
whose seed was in itself after his kind: and God saw that
it was good. And the evening and the morning were the
third day.*

*And God said, Let there be lights in the firmament of the
heaven to divide the day from the night; and let them be
for signs and seasons, and for days and years: And let
them be for lights in the firmament of the heaven to give
light upon the earth: and it was so. And God made two
great lights: the greater light to rule the day, and the
lesser light to rule the night: he made the stars also...and
God saw that it was good. And the evening and the
morning were the fourth day.*

And God said, Let the waters bring forth abundantly the moving creature that hath life, and fowl that may fly above the earth in the open firmament of heaven. And God created great whales, and every living creature that moveth, which the waters brought forth abundantly, after their kind, and every winged fowl after his kind: and God saw that it was good. And God blessed them saying, Be fruitful and multiply, and fill the waters and the seas, and let the fowl multiply in the earth. And the morning and the evening were the fifth day.

And God said, Let the earth bring forth the living creature after his kind, cattle and creeping thing, and beast of the earth after his kind: and it was so...And God saw that it was good. And God said, Let us make man in our image, after our likeness...So God created man in his own image, in the image of God created he him; male and female created he them. And God blessed them and God said unto them, Be fruitful and multiply, and replenish the earth and subdue it: and have dominion over the fish of the sea, and over the fowl of the air, and over every living thing that moveth over the earth. And God said, Behold, I have given you every herb bearing seed, which is upon the face of all the earth, end every tree, in the which is the fruit of a tree yielding seed; to you it shall be for meat. And to every beast of the earth, and to every fowl of the air, and to every thing that creepeth upon the earth wherein there is life, I have given every green herb for meat: and it was so. And God saw everything that he had made, and, behold, it was very good. And the evening and the morning were the sixth day.

Thus the heavens and the earth were finished, and the all the host of them. And on the seventh day God ended his work which he had made; and he rested on the seventh day from all his work which he had made.

Genesis *1:1 - 2:3*

Appendix B:
Bringing Light Into The Darkness:
The Principle of Positive Intention

by Robert B. Dilts

One of the most important but often misunderstood (and therefore controversial) principles of NLP is that of *'positive intention'*. Simply put, the principle states that at some level all behavior is (or at one time was) "positively intended". Another way to say it is that all behavior serves (or at one time served) a 'positive purpose'.

The positive intention behind 'aggressive' behavior, for example, is often 'protection'. The positive intention or purpose behind 'fear' is usually 'safety'. The positive purpose behind anger can be to 'maintain boundaries'. 'Hatred' may have the positive purpose of 'motivating' a person to take action. The positive intentions behind something like 'resistance to change' could encompass a range of issues; including the desire to acknowledge, honor or respect the past; the need to protect oneself by staying with the familiar, and the attempt to hold onto the positive things one has had in the past, and so on.

Even physical symptoms may serve a positive purpose. NLP views any symptom, including physical symptoms, as a communication that something is not functioning appropriately. Physical symptoms often signal to people that something is out of balance. Sometimes physical symptoms are even a sign that something is being healed.

Sometimes a particular problem behavior or symptom may even serve multiple positive intentions. I have worked with people who wanted to quit smoking, for instance, who discovered that it served many positive purposes. They smoked in the morning in order to "wake up". They smoked during the day in order to "reduce stress," "concentrate" and, paradoxi-

cally, "remember to breathe." They smoked at night in order
to "relax." Often, smoking served to cover up or 'cloud'
negative emotions. Perhaps most importantly, smoking was
the one thing that they did "just for themselves" to bring
some pleasure into their lives.

Another basic principle of NLP, that is related to that of
positive intention, is that it is useful to separate one's
"behavior" from one's "self" - that is, to separate the positive
intent, function, belief, etc., that generates a behavior from
the behavior itself. In other words, it is more respectful,
ecological and productive to respond to the 'deep structure'
than to the surface expression of a problematic behavior.

A consequence of combining this principle with the principle of positive intention is that in order to change behavior
or establish viable alternatives, the new choices must in
some way satisfy the positive purpose of the previous behavior. When the positive intentions and purposes of a problem
state or symptom have not been satisfied, then, ironically,
even "normal" or "desired" behaviors can produce equally
problematic or pathological results. A person who stops
being aggressive, for instance, but has no other way to
protect himself or herself, just exchanges one set of problems
for another. Quitting the behavior of smoking without finding
alternatives for all of the important purposes that it serves
can lead a person into a nightmare of new problems.

According to another basic NLP principle - that of 'pacing
and leading' - effective change would first involve 'pacing' by
acknowledging the positive intentions behind the existing
behavior. 'Leading' would involve assisting the individual to
widen his or her map of the world in order to find more
appropriate choices for successfully achieving those positive
intentions. These choices would allow the person to preserve
the positive intention or purpose through different means.
This is what the various NLP techniques of 'reframing'
attempt to accomplish.

Why people object to the principle of positive intention.

On one hand, the principle of positive intention - and the approach to change described above - seem quite natural and effective. Yet, the notion of 'positive intention' has also engendered much criticism and ridicule; even by some members of the NLP community. The objections range from the perception that it is more theoretical and philosophical than practical, to the belief that it is downright dangerous. One of the purposes of this article is to acknowledge and address some of these concerns.

The notion of 'positive intention' is more philosophical than scientific. It can't be proved.

Actually, the principle of positive intention does not come from religious or romantic idealism, but rather from the scientific discipline of systems theory. The fundamental premise of the principle of positive intent is that systems (especially self organizing or "cybernetic" systems) are geared toward *adaptation*. That is, there is a built in tendency to optimize some important elements in the system or to keep the system in balance. Thus, the ultimate purpose of all actions, responses or behaviors within a system is 'adaptive' - or was adaptive given the context in which those behaviors were initially established.

It is true that you cannot objectively 'prove' that there *really* is a positive intention behind a particular behavior; that is why it is considered a 'presupposition'. It is something that is presupposed, not proved. Similarly, one cannot 'prove' that the 'map is not the territory' and that 'there is no one right map of the world'. These are part of the basic 'epistemology' of NLP - they are the basic beliefs upon which the rest of the model is based.

NLP principles and presuppositions are like the fundamental concepts of Euclidian geometry. For instance, Euclid built his geometry upon the concept of the 'point'. A point is defined as 'an entity that has a position but no other properties'-it has no size, no mass, no color, no shape. It is of course impossible to prove that a point *really* has no size, mass, color, etc. However, if you accept this presupposition, along with a few others, you can build a whole system of geometry. The conclusions of this system can then be 'proved' with respect to their adherence to the fundamental but unproven concepts. It is important to realize that one does not have to accept Euclid's assumption about a point in order to create a geometry. There are other geometries based on different presuppositions. [For instance, MIT mathematician Seymour Pappert (1980) built his fascinating 'Turtle geometry' for children substituting the notion of a 'Turtle' for a 'point'; a 'Turtle' being an entity that has a position *and* a direction.]

Thus, accepting the principle of 'positive intention' is ultimately an act of faith. And in many ways, the notion of positive intention is probably the 'spiritual' core of NLP. If we accept that there are positive intentions behind every behavior, then we will find or create them as opposed to waiting for the proof that such intentions exist.

If people supposedly have positive intentions then why do they do such bad things?

It is common wisdom that "The road to hell is paved with good intentions." Having a good intention is not a guarantee of good behavior. People who have good intentions do bad things because they have limited maps of the world. Problems arise when a well intended person's map of the world presents only a few choices for satisfying their intentions.

This is why it is important to consider the principle of positive intention in relation to the other teachings of NLP. Isolated from the other NLP presuppositions and the technology of NLP, the principle of positive intention would indeed be naive idealism. Without the mastery of the NLP change techniques, thinking tools, communication skills etc., it would be irrelevant whether someone had a positive intention or not because we would be helpless to direct their attention to a new behavior anyway. As Einstein pointed out, "You cannot solve a problem with the same type of thinking that is creating it." The principle of positive intention must be coupled with powerful and effective creativity and problem solving skills.

It is also important to keep in mind that people can only have a positive intention for the particular part of the total system that they are aware of or identify with. Thus, an individual who is knowingly and 'purposefully' doing something harmful to another, will often have a positive intention for himself or herself which does not include the other. In fact, the concept of 'negative intentions' probably stems from this kind of experience.

The positive intention behind the belief in negative intention and the rejection of the notion of 'positive intention' is undoubtedly "protection." People who reject the notion of positive intention are often afraid of either being or appearing 'naive'. They also often feel helpless to change anything. Without the mastery of the appropriate NLP skills, people simply end up feeling, "If they were really positively intended they would have changed by now."

It is important, however, not to confuse the notion that people are motivated by 'positive intentions' with the idea that people are always able to keep in mind the 'best interests' of others or the rest of the system. The fact that others are positively intended does not automatically make them wise or capable of being altruistic - these are the result of intelligence, skill and their map of the world. Adolph Hitler had a very positive intention - for the part of the system that he identified with.

A mugger who robs and perhaps even kills another to get money has a positive intention for himself but no identification with the victim. The European pioneers who killed

Native American fathers and their families in order to protect their own families had a positive intention but had limited choices. In their map the 'red devils' were not human. The Native American warriors who killed European fathers and their families in order to protect their hunting grounds had a very positive intention, but had limited choices. They both lacked the skills to communicate effectively with one another, and their maps of the world did not allow them to appreciate and manage the cultural differences between them.

Doesn't accepting that a behavior comes from a positive intention make that behavior alright?

The fact that some action or symptom may have a positive intention behind it does not justify the behavior or make it acceptable or "OK." Rather, the principle of positive intention states what is necessary to be able to permanently change a behavior or resolve a symptom or resistance. The principle of positive intention addresses issues of 'change', 'healing' and 'ecology' more so than 'morality' or 'justice'. It is more about the future than the past. The principle of positive intention merely asserts that healing or "associative correction" involves adding new choices to the individual's impoverished model of the world. These new choices would need to be able to satisfy the positive intention or purpose that the individual is (consciously or unconsciously) attempting to fulfill, but not have the negative or pathological consequences of the problem behavior or symptom.

But I can't find any positive purpose to some behaviors.

Positive intentions are not always conscious nor obvious. Because we are not used to thinking in terms of positive intentions, it is sometimes difficult to find them right away and therefore we find it easier to lapse into other explanations for a behavior or symptom. But if one is committed to finding them and looks deeply enough, they will be there.

Sometimes the intention or 'deep structure' is far removed from the surface level behavior. In these cases, the relation between the intention and behavior may seem paradoxical. For instance, I have worked with suicidal people whose positive intention is to "attain peace." Parents sometimes physically punish or even abuse their children to "show them that they love them." The mystery of the seemingly paradoxical relationship between the positive intention and the resulting behavior lies in the past events and model of the world in which the relationship was formed.

Another conclusion of combining the principle of positive intention with other NLP presuppositions is that any behavior no matter how 'evil', 'crazy' or 'bizarre' it seems, is or was the best choice available to the person at that point in time, given his or her model of the world. That is, all behavior is or was perceived as necessary or appropriate (from the 'actor's' point of view) given the context in which it was established. What happens many times, however, is that the positive intention for which the behavior was established is no longer actually being served by the behavior. As an example, the positive intention behind 'revenge' is often initially to "put things right" in order to try to heal them. Instead it creates an unending or escalating feud (like the Hatfields and McCoys). To truly heal the situation it is necessary to break the cycle by finding a way of thinking that is different from that which is creating the problem.

What is important to keep in mind is that, even though the situation in which the problematic response was established is now outdated, the positive intention behind it, or the purpose which it was intended to serve, may still be valid and important to acknowledge and address.

What if I can't find any positive purpose in the past?

In some situations the positive function of a symptom or behavior was not part of the initiating circumstances but was rather established later as a 'secondary gain'. For instance, a person may not have intended to become physically sick, but nonetheless received a lot of attention and relief from his or her responsibilities when he or she did become ill. This attention and relief, received as a positive by-product of the illness, could become a secondary gain - indicating areas of imbalance in the person's 'normal' life that need to be addressed. If they are not adequately dealt with, the person may be likely to relapse.

But when I make people aware of perfectly good alternatives they don't always accept them.

It is important to keep in mind at this point that there is a subtle but significant difference between 'alternatives' and 'choices'. 'Alternatives' are external to a person. 'Choices' are alternatives that have become a part of the person's map. An individual could be given many options or alternatives but really have no choice. Choice involves having the capability and the contextual cues to be able to internally select the most appropriate option.

In NLP, it is also considered important that the person possess more than one other alternative besides the symptom or problematic response. There is a saying in NLP that "One choice is no choice at all. Two choices is a dilemma. It is not until a person has three possibilities that he or she is really able to legitimately choose."

What about when someone admits that he or she has other choices but is still doing the same thing?

What often confuses people about the principle of positive intention is that it seems the person "should know better." They should have the intelligence or maturity to employ other alternatives to achieve their desired intentions. It is not uncommon for a people to say over and over again that they realize something is not good for them or achieving what they really want or intend, yet still persist in the behavior.

The influence of past events often extends beyond the specific memory of the particular situation. Under certain conditions, events can produce altered states of consciousness which lead to a "splitting of consciousness," such that a part of the person's thinking process became disassociated from the rest. This disassociated part of consciousness, what Freud called a "secondary consciousness", could produce ideas which were "very intense but are cut off from associative communication with the rest of the content of consciousness."

In the view of NLP, people are always drifting or moving between various states of consciousness. There is a wide variety of states which the nervous system is capable of achieving. In fact, from the NLP perspective, it is useful and desirable to have 'parts'. In circumstances that require high levels of performance, for instance, people often place themselves mentally and physically into states that are different from their "normal state" of consciousness. Certain tasks require that individuals use their body and nervous system in special ways. For instance, athletic performances, labor and birth experiences, even tasks requiring high levels of concentration like surgery, are often accompanied by special states. The ideas, perceptions and thoughts that occur in these states can be "associated amongst themselves" more easily than experiences that occur in other states or circumstances. This kind of process is one of the ways that we keep from being overwhelmed by the vast contents of our experiences.

The degree of influence of a particular 'part' depends upon the 'level' at which it has been formed. Some parts are more at the capability level; like a 'creative' part, a 'logical' part or an 'intuitive' part. Other parts are more at the level of beliefs and values; such as a part that 'values health more than success' or a part that believes 'family is more important than career'. Still others may be at the level of identity; such as a part that is an 'adult' versus a part that is a 'child'.

Different 'parts' may have different intentions, purposes and capabilities that may or may not be connected to other parts of a person and to his or her normal state of consciousness. Thus, while one part of a person may understand something, another part may not. One part of a person may believe something is important while another part may believe it is unnecessary. As a result, an individual may have different parts with different intentions. These intentions may come into conflict with one another, or lead to behaviors that seem bizarre and irrational to others and even to part of a person's own consciousness.

In other words, the fact that the "normal consciousness" of a person recognizes other choices does not mean that the "secondary consciousness" that is initiating the behavior understands or accepts those choices. A symptom is only completely 'reframed' when the part of the person that is generating the problematic response is identified, the positive intention behind the response understood and acknowledged, and when other effective choices for achieving the positive intention have been internalized by that part. (The specifics of how to conduct such communications have been detailed in a number of NLP books including *Roots of NLP, Frogs Into Princes, Solutions, NLP Volume I, Reframing*.)

Are you saying that there is no such thing as 'evil'?

The notion of 'evil' is certainly an ancient one. Yet, perhaps surprisingly to some, it has not always existed as an essential part of human consciousness. In his book *The Origin of Consciousness in the Breakdown of the Bicameral Mind* (1976), Julian Jaynes points out that references to the concept of "evil" do not appear in ancient writings or artifacts (Greek, Egyptian or Hebrew) until around 1200 BC. According to Jaynes, in order for the idea of "evil" to arise, people's behavior had to become perceived as being sufficiently disassociated from the will of the various gods that controlled them in order for people to have their own 'free will'. It was only with advent of ongoing contact and interaction between peoples of different cultures, and the resulting belief that the differences in people's behaviors came from their own internal thoughts and wills, that ideas such as 'deception' and 'evil' emerged. Without individual consciousness and will there can be no intent, positive or negative. It would seem that, historically, the concept of evil arose out of our struggle to understand and come to terms with our own internal programming.

Even from the earliest times, however, 'evil' was associated with 'darkness' and 'good' was associated with 'light'. Destructive and harmful behaviors come from 'darkness'. Loving and healing behaviors come from 'light'. This metaphor fits in very well with the NLP notion of positive intention. Positive intentions are like light. Their purpose is to bring illumination and warmth to the world. Symptoms and problematic behaviors emerge out of the darkness - the places that the light is unable to reach.

It is very important to realize, however, that 'darkness' is not a 'force', it is merely the absence of light. Light can shine into darkness, but darkness cannot 'shine' into light. Thus, the relationship between light and the shadow that it casts is not one of a struggle between opposing forces. The question is, "What is obstructing the light?" and "How can we get some light to where it needs to be?"

From an NLP perspective, 'darkness' comes from a narrow map of the world or from something in that model of the world that is interfering with the 'light' of the positive intention and casting a shadow. Change comes from 'widening the aperture' of the person's map of the world or by finding and transforming the obstacles to the light - not by attacking the shadow. According to NLP, the obstacles to the light come from limiting beliefs or 'thought viruses' in our mental maps of the world. Typically, these obstacles come as beliefs or assumptions which stand in opposition to the basic NLP presuppositions.

For example, consider just how easy it is to create conflict and violence by taking on the following beliefs: "There is only one true map of the world. They (the chosen enemy) have the wrong map of the world - I/we have the correct map of the world. They are negatively intended - they want to hurt us. They are incapable of changing - I/we have tried everything I/we could. They are not part of our system - they are fundamentally different from us."

These beliefs, taken together, have no doubt been at the heart of every atrocity that has been committed in human history. The fundamental 'light' and healing capacity of NLP comes from its commitment to promote a different set of presuppositions:

"We are a system that is part of a much larger system. This system is fundamentally geared towards health and adaptation. Therefore, we are all ultimately motivated by positive intentions. Our maps of the world, however, are limited and don't always provide us with all the possible choices. We are, nonetheless, capable of changing, and once we are able to perceive a truly viable option, we will automatically take it. The issue is to be able to widen one's model of the world to include other choices and capabilities for protection and wisdom and to assist others in doing so as well."

It is clearly these types of beliefs that have brought an end to the Cold War, brought down the Berlin Wall and that will hopefully one day bring peace to Ireland and the Middle East. It is the manifestation of these presuppositions that has been one of the main missions and contributions of NLP.

Appendix C:
Spiritual Reunion -
Dealing With Separation, Loss
and Grief

by Robert B. Dilts

The experiences of separation, loss and grief are an important reminder of the need for spiritual awareness and connection in our lives. The following process applies a number of the principles and "tools" that we have been exploring in this book to help transform the sense of loss and grief into appreciation and gratitude.

I developed these steps as a result of reflecting on the process I went through at the time my mother was dying in December, 1996. While the 'Spritual Reunion' procedure may be used to help with the experience of loss or grief brought about by physical death, people have also reported relief from the types of negative emotions triggered by other forms of loss, such as divorce or long term geographical separation.

The steps of the process are:

1. Identify and associate into the experience of separation, sadness or grief.

2. Step away from that experience and go to a centered and resourceful state in which you are aligned and wise.

3. Choose two mentors to be your guardian angels. Select mentors you know will always be a part of you.

4. With your hands, sculpt a life size "hologram" of the person you are missing. Create the person as you want him or her to be.

If there are any negative or painful memories, put them on balloons and let them go. (Images can go on the outside of the balloon, voices and sounds can go inside the balloon.)

5. Breathe life into the hologram and give your new mentor the voice you would like him or her to have.

6. Ask the new mentor, "What is the gift you have been wanting to give me all this time?" Go to "second position" with your new mentor, by putting yourself into his or her shoes, and answer the questions. Create a symbol for the gift (e.g., a golden heart).

7. Return to "first position," by associating back into yourself, and answer the question, "What is my gift for you?" Create a symbol of your gift to the other person (e.g., a fountain pen that writes in many colors).

8. Exchange gifts with your new mentor and connect your hearts with an eternal silver thread of light.

9. Honor the gift you have received by finding someone else in your life to share it with. Future pace how you will share this gift and keep it alive. Use your new mentor as a resource to help you share this gift.

10. Imagine your new mentor being welcomed by your other mentors.

11. Bring your gift, your new mentor and your other "guardian angels" into the situation in which you had previously experienced separation, sadness or grief, and notice how your experience is transformed.

Bibliography

Angels Fear: Towards an Epistemology of the Sacred, Gregory and Mary Catherine Bateson, Bantam Books, New York, N.Y., 1988.

Belonging to the Universe, Capra et al.; Harper Collins, San Francisco, CA, 1995.

A Brief History of Everything, Wilber, Ken; Shambala, Boulder, CO, 1995.

Beliefs; Pathways to Health and Well-Being, Dilts, R., Halbom, T. Smith, S.; Metamorphous Press, Portland, OR, 1990.

Change Your Mind, Andreas, S., Andreas, C., Real People Press, Moab, Utah, 1987.

Changing Belief Systems with NLP, Dilts, R., Meta Publications, Capitola, CA, 1990.

Cognitive Patterns of Jesus of Nazareth; Dilts, R., Dynamic Learning Publications, Ben Lomond, CA, 1992.

A Course In Miracles; Foundation for Inner Peace, Tiburon, CA, 1985.

Frogs into Princes, Bandler, R. and Grinder, J.; Real People Press, Moab, Utah, 1979.

Grace and Grit, Wilber, Ken; Shambala, Boulder, CO, 1991.

Heart of the Mind, Andreas, C. & Andreas, S.; Real People Press, Moab, Utah, 1989.

The Holy Bible, Thomas Nelson Inc., Nashville, TN, 1976.

Homecoming, Bradshaw, J.; Bantam Books, New York,NY, 1992.

Introducing Neuro-Linguistic Programming, O'Connor, J., Seymour, J., Aquarian Press, Cornwall, England, 1990.

Lazy Man's Guide to Enlightenment, Golas, T., Bantam Books, New York, NY, 1980.

Mind and Nature, Bateson, Gregory; E. P. Dutton, New York, NY, 1979.

My Pathway to Wholeness; Dilts, P., Dynamic Learning Publications, Ben Lomond, CA, 1992.

NLP: The New Technology of Achievement, Andreas, S. and Faulkner, C. (Ed.s), William Morrow And Company, Inc., New York, NY, 1994.

ReFraming, Bandler, R. and Grinder, J.; Real People Press, Moab, Utah, 1982.

Riding the Horse Backwards, Mindell, A. and Mindell, A.; Penguin Books, New York, NY, 1994.

Steps To an Ecology of Mind, Bateson, G.; Ballantine Books, New York, New York, 1972.

Strategies of Genius Vols I - III, Dilts, R., Meta Publications, Capitola, Ca.,1994.

Turtles All The Way Down: Prerequisites to Personal Genius, DeLozier, J. & Grinder, J., Metamorphous Press, Portland, OR, 1987.

Visionary Leadership Skills: Creating A World To Which People Want To Belong, Dilts, R., Meta Publications, Capitola, CA,1996.

Index

A

Acceptance 99
Addiction 129
Agony 97
Alignment 24
Amazing Grace 257
An Emotional and Spiritual
    Vocabulary 242
Anchoring 48
Anchors 57
"And Then a Miracle Happens" 7
Andreas, Connirae 129
Anger 97
Anne Frank 253
Archetype 112
Archetype Patterns 112, 160
"Archetypic" Mother and Father
    146
Arrien, Angeles 252
Attaching The Shadow To Its
    "Spiritually Evolving
    Essence" 121
Authenticity 242
Autumn 172
Awareness 243

B

Basic Elements of Healing 83
Bateson, Gregory 4, 18, 255,
    168
Behavior 18 - 20, 22, 26, 27, 40
Behaviors 49
Belief 28, 29, 169
Belief Change 169
Belief System 18, 40
Beliefs 22, 40, 170, 205

Beliefs and Values 19, 20, 28, 49
Bethlehem 168
Bible 65
Bird Dream 13
Birth 242, 166, 172
Blake, William 255
Body 14, 40, 109
Bohm, David 246
'Breath of Life' 119
Buddha 250

C

Capabilities 19, 20, 22
Capability 27
Capra, Fritjof 89
Castaneda, Carlos 255
Change 239, 169
Changing in the Twinkling of an
    Eye 89
Checking For Objections To
    Releasing The Shadow 120
Cherry Tree 168, 169
Childbirth 95
Christ 259, 233, 234
Closing Ritual 233
Co-Alignment 24, 34, 35
Co-dependence 129
Compassion 252, 94
Concentration Camps 253
Connecting With The "Spiritually
    Evolving" Self 122
Consciousness 253
Course In Miracles 144, 252
Creating Symbols 179
Crown of the Head 42
cummings, e. e. 234, 258

Currently Embodying   177, 182
Cycle of Spiritual Change   191
Cycles   169, 171, 175
Cycles of Change   169

D

Dalai Lama   253
Darkness   134
Death   242, 88, 89, 101, 108,
   166
Deeper Structure   52, 169
Depression   97
Despair   97
Developmental Cycles   171
Diaphragm   40
Discovering The Shadow   112
Discovering The "Spiritually
   Evolving" Essence of The
   Shadow   119
Dissociation   97
Divine   247
Drawings   44
Duckling   146, 147

E

Egg   157, 158, 161
Einstein, Albert   4, 254, 137, 235
Emperor's Looking-Glass   135
Emphasis on Experience   10
Enemies   16
Enmeshment   110, 114, 126 - 130
Environment   18 - 20, 22, 24,
   25, 39
Epstein, Todd   50
Eternity   56, 58
Ethics   244
Exploring the Structure of the
   Shadow   114
Eyes   53, 54, 56

F

Faith   243, 253, 261
Family History   161
Family Secrets   138
Father   147, 149, 150, 152
   154, 155, 158 161
Father's Father   158
Fear   15, 144, 145, 242, 252
Fear and Love   144, 145
Final Drawings of the Large "S"
   Self   232
Finding the Positive Purpose of
   the Shadow Attachment   116
Finite   246
First Position   66, 71, 74, 80,
   81, 107, 200
First Position Future   201, 225
First Position Past   228
First Position Present   225 - 230
Flexibility   241
Forehead   41
Forgive and Forget   142
Forgive and Learn   145
Forgive and Remember   144
Forgiveness   60, 144, 145, 242
Form Versus Content   130
Forms of Enmeshment   111
Fort Ord   62
Fox, Matthew   252
Frankl, Viktor   254
Freedom   254, 256
Fruits of the Spirit   4, 107
Future Observer   202, 213, 227
Future Other   202, 211, 226
Future Self   202, 209, 225

G

Generative Change   206
Generative NLP   200, 223, 225
"Generative" Processes   206
Genesis   263

"Genesis Pattern" 224
Getting New Perspectives on
    Your Life 205
Gide, Andre 252
Gift 118, 126, 151, 152, 156
    158, 161
Gift of the Father 152, 153
Gift of the Mother 151, 154
Gift of the New Integration of
    Mother and Father 156
Goals 254
God 243, 248, 255, 89, 108,
    109, 112, 234
God's thoughts 4
Golas, Thaddeus 252, 98
Golden Rule 253
Goodbye 137, 138
Grace 15, 64, 65, 242
Grace and Grit 247
Grandfather 158
Grandmother 158
Gratitude 242
Great Grandmother 158
Greetings 166, 167
Grief 101, 277
Guardian Angel 70, 72 - 77

H

Healing 57, 58, 65, 83, 252
Healing 'Energy' 42
Healing Relationships 65
Heart 40, 105
Heaven 98
Hegel, Georg 256
Hell 98
Hinduism 252
Hokey Pokey 6, 54, 56
Holocaust 145
Honoring the Shadow's Proper
    Place 178, 185
Human Being 252, 236
Humility 242

Hurt 94, 95, 97, 242
Hymn 168

I

'I Messages' 11
Ideals 253
Identity 18 - 20, 23, 29, 41,
    88, 178
Impeccability 5
Imprint 147
Imprinting 146
"Imprinting" and the Self
    Parenting Process 146
Individual Mind 255
Infinite 246, 252
Innocence 145
Integrating the Mother and the
    Father 154
Integrating Time Frames 58
Integration 155, 156, 159,
    161, 162
Integration of Mother and
    Father 156
Intention 83
Intentions 57, 58
Introductions 44

J

Jesus 51, 169, 207
Joseph 168
Judgments 25
Jung, Carl 253

K

Knowledge 254

L

Landscape 200, 201, 205, 206
"Landscape" for Spiritual
    Transformation 176

Large "S" Self   13, 42 -44, 46,
    108, 172, 175 - 177, 180, 232
Larger Mind   255
Larger System   30
Lazy Man's Guide to
    Enlightenment 98
Leprosy 93
Letting Go of the
    Unnecessary   88, 178
Level 21
Level Co-Alignment   24, 35
Levels   18, 22
Levels of Experience   18, 22
Levine, Stephen   252
Life 252
Life Cycles   171
Life Landscape   200, 224
Light   101, 134
Logical Level Co-Alignment
    Process 35
Love   9, 15, 98, 106, 108, 112,
    130, 133, 144, 145, 243,
    252, 253
Loving Anyway   103, 105, 106
Lower Belly   40
Luminous Beings   255

M

Magical Hands   114 -116, 118,
    121, 122, 126
Manifestations of Spirit 4
Map and Territory 46
Maps of the World   236, 239
Mary and Joseph 168
Matter 256
McDonald, Bill   103, 104
Meaning   100, 101
Meaningful and Meaningless
    Pain 92, 95, 96
Meaningless Pain 97
Meister Eckhart 254
Mental Characteristics   254

Mercy   60, 61, 65, 242, 252
Message   99, 100
Message Value   93, 100
Meta-Outcomes   132, 161
Metaphor   29, 78, 82, 222 230
Mind   255, 40
Miracle   7, 8, 252
Misery 97
Mission 41
Mogadishu 102
Monk And The Tiger   139
Monterey   62, 63, 64
Morality 244
Mother   147 - 149, 151, 153 -
    155, 158, 160, 161
Mother Teresa 253
Mother's Mother 158
Multiple Dissociations 97
Museum of Personal History
    178, 185, 186
'My Friend John' and the Tiger
    142

N

Necessary Pain   100
"Neuro-Logical" Levels   22, 23
Neurological 'Circuitry' 22
Never Ending Story   175
NLP   4, 22, 46, 48, 50, 88,
    239, 243
Non-Violent Change Work   129
Nonliteral Language   169
Now   52, 53
Now and Forever 57
Numbness   97, 98

O

Objections   131
Objections To Releasing The
    Shadow   120
Observer Position   110

Ojibway 253
On Defining the Spirit 244
Opening to Letting Go of the
	Unnecessary 178, 184
Opening to Spiritual Awakening
	177, 181
Opening To The Shadow 107,
	172
Overtor, Patrick 261

P

Pain 92 - 97, 99, 100, 242,
	252, 253,
"Pain" and "Hurt" 94
Palestine 169
Part 116, 117, 119, 120
Past Observer 204, 220, 230
Past Other 204, 218, 229
Past Self 203, 204, 216, 229
Peace 253
Perceptual Positions 66, 200,
	207
Perennial Philosophy 247
Pity 253
Positive Intention 16, 145
Positive Purpose 116, 118,
	126, 127, 129, 236
Possession 252
Practicing the Spiritual Renewal
	Process 224
Presence of Eternity 48, 52,
	58, 172, 207
Present 52, 58
Present Observer 203, 215, 228
Present Other 203, 214, 227
Present Self 201, 203, 204, 208
Presuppositions of NLP 239
Proper Place of the Shadow 124
Psoriasis 99
Psychic 244

R

Readings 233, 237, 258
Rebirth 159, 161, 162, 166,
	169, 170 - 172, 243
Relationship 51, 83, 84
Relationships 65
Releasing Enmeshment 186
Releasing Enmeshment as a Path
	to Spiritual Growth 133
Releasing Enmeshment With
	The Shadow 114, 125, 126,
	129, 130, 132, 133, 134,
	172, 208
Releasing The Connection With
	The Shadow 121
Releasing The Shadow 120
Religion 245, 253
"Remedial" work 206
Remen, Rachel Naomi 245
Resource 224
Resources 205
Respect 121, 133
Ritual 8, 83, 242
Rituals 84
Robert Dilts' Story 192
Robert McDonald's Story 195
Rumi 252, 260

S

Sacred Journey Process 38,
	39, 172, 207
Sacred Space 175, 178, 187
Saint Theresa 253
Satir, Virginia 253
Saying Goodbye 137, 138
Schweitzer, Albert 252
Second Position 67, 75, 76, 81,
	200
Second Position Future 226,
	227
Second Position Past 229

Second Position Present 227
Seeds 207
Self 12
Self Parenting Process 146 -148,
    160
Self Position 108
Sensory Perception 25
Serve 252
Shadow 91, 98, 101 - 103, 107,
    109 -114, 116, 117, 121,
    122, 124, 126, 127, 129, 131
    - 133, 145, 166, 172, 175 -
    177, 183, 186, 207
Shadow Attachment 114, 116
Shadows and Light 101
Siegel, Bernie 89
Significant Other 205
Silence 6
Silly Greetings 166
Sin 242
Skillful Presence 27
Skills 28
Small "s" and Large "S" Self 12
Small "s" Self 45, 177, 182, 249
Somalia 102
Soul 255
Sower and the Seeds 207
Sperm 157, 158, 161
Spirit 256, 108, 109
Spiritual 18, 20, 23, 30, 243,
    244
Spiritual Awakening 166, 172
Spiritual Awareness 100
Spiritual Birth 12
Spiritual Bliss 98
Spiritual Depth 94
Spiritual Energy 42
Spiritual Experience 11, 49, 68
Spiritual Expression of the
    Three Basic Perceptual
    Positions 69
Spiritual Growth 133

Spiritual Healing 243, 172
Spiritual Healing Process 68,
    80, 207
Spiritual Practice 243
Spiritual Renewal 200, 207,
    230
Spiritual Renewal Grid 200
Spiritual Renewal Process
    206, 208, 223, 225
Spiritual Wholeness 68, 70, 72,
    74, 76 - 78, 80, 82, 166,
    172, 207
"Spiritually Evolving" Essence of
    the Shadow 119, 121
Spiritually Evolving Self 118 -
    120, 122, 123, 126, 128,
    130, 131
Springtime 172, 173
Stories 168, 173
Story of the King and Queen 60
Storytelling 174
Suffering 93 - 95, 97, 99, 242
Suicide 101, 103, 104, 105,
    170
Summer 172
Surface Structure 52
Symbol 29, 42, 78, 109, 110,
    112, 149, 150, 156, 177
Symbol of the Father 149
Symbol of the Mother 148
Symbolic Rebirth Cycle 169,
    173, 175, 191, 208
Symbolic Rebirth Worksheet
    177, 198
Symbols 169, 173, 179
Symeon The New Theologian
    259, 233
Systems 240

T

Telling Your Story 189
The Finite and The Infinite 246

The Map is not the Territory 239
The Two Lines Into Heaven 10
The Wise Rabbi 5
Thich Nhat Hahn 252
Third Position 67, 77, 81, 107, 201
Third Position Future 226
Third Position Past 230
Third Position Present 228
"Those Who Have Ears To Hear" 198
Thoughts 40
Throat 41
Tiger 139, 140, 142, 143
Time 48
Time Lines 48, 49, 200, 201
Tools Of The Spirit 243
Transcendent Love 144
True Love 253
Truth 242

U

U.S. Army 62
Unconscious Mind 198
Uniting the Large "S" and Small "s" Selves 14
Universe 235, 236
Unmerited Mercy 62, 65
Unnecessary Suffering 95, 99
Upper Legs 39

V

Values 18, 254
Varieties of Spiritual Experience 68
Viet Nam War 62
Vision 30, 31

W

Walking Through the Cycle of Spiritual Change 191

What do you want? 88
Wholeness 159
Wilber, Ken 247
Winter 172
Wisdom 99
Womb 157, 161

Y

Yearning for Spiritual Wholeness 177, 179

Z

Zen 250

Afterword

We hope you have enjoyed this exploration into *Tools of the Spirit*. As we indicated during the course of the book, we conduct seminars on *Tools of the Spirit* throughout the world. We have also developed an extension of *Tools of the Spirit* for teams and groups entitled *Group Mind - Team Spirit: Wisdom in Action*. The focus of this program is on creating a context for the emergence and evolution of personal genius. We also create and conduct, individually and together, training programs on other applications of NLP including, Creativity, Health, Leadership, Presentations Skills, Brief Therapy, Belief Change and Modeling.

If you would like to receive further information regarding these programs and any future developments related to *Tools of the Spirit*, please contact:

Robert Dilts
P.O. Box 67448
Scotts Valley, California 95067-7448
Phone: (408) 438-8314
Fax: (408) 438-8571
email: rdilts@nlpu.com

Robert McDonald
366 Hihn Street
Felton, California 95018
Phone: (408) 335-3727
Fax: (408) 335-5919
email: robert@mettanlp.com

Anchor Point Productions
346 S. 500 E. #200
Salt Lake City, Utah 84102-4022
Phone: (801) 534-1022
Fax : (801) 532-2113
email: info@nlpanchorpoint.com

About the Authors

Robert McDonald   **Robert Dilts**

Robert B. Dilts

Mr. Dilts has been a developer, author, trainer and consultant in the field of *Neuro-Linguistic Programming* (NLP) since 1975. In addition to spearheading the applications of NLP to health, learning, creativity and organizational development, his personal contributions to the field of NLP include much of the seminal work on the NLP techniques of Strategies and Belief Systems, and the development of what has become known as "Systemic NLP." Some of his techniques and models include: Reimprinting, Integration of Conflicting Beliefs, Sleight of Mouth Patterns, The Spelling Strategy, The Allergy Technique, Neuro-Logical Levels, The Belief Change Cycle, Generative NLP Patterns, the Unified Field Theory for NLP and many others.

Dilts is the principle author of **Neuro-Linguistic Programming Vol. I,** and has authored numerous other books on NLP including **Changing Belief Systems with NLP** and **Beliefs: Pathways to Health and Well Being** (co-authored with Tim Hallbom and Suzi Smith) which describe his work in changing limiting beliefs and creating functional belief systems. **Tools for Dreamers** (co-authored with Todd Epstein) and **Skills for the Future**, explore the applications of NLP to manage and enhance creativity. **Effective Presentation Skills** covers the key communication and relational skills necessary for successful public speaking. His work, **Strategies of Genius Vols. I, II & III**, applies the tools of NLP to model the thinking processes of important historical figures; such as Aristotle, Sir Arthur Conan Doyle's Sherlock Holmes, Walt Disney, Mozart, Albert Einstein, Sigmund Freud, Leonardo da Vinci and Nikola Tesla. **Dynamic Learning** (co-authored with Todd Epstein), explores the structure of effective learning strategies and the applications of NLP in education. His recent work, **Visionary Leadership Skills**, studies tools and skills necessary for "creating a world to which people want to belong."

He has been a founder or co-founder of a number of successful professional organizations and companies including *NLP University, The Institute for the Advanced Studies of Health (IASH), The Academy of Behavioral Technology, The Dynamic Learning Center, Behavioral Engineering* and *NeuroLink International.*

Robert McDonald, M.S.

Robert McDonald is an internationally acclaimed author, trainer, speaker and consultant. He holds an M.S. in Counseling and Mental Health, and has created and presented seminars on interpersonal communication and mental health skills for over 25 years. On the business front, he co-authored **NLP: The New Technology of Achievement** (with Steve

Andreas, et al) and *Success Mastery With NLP* (Nightingale-Conant audio tapes with Charles Faulkner).

His contributions to psychology, NLP, and Psychoteleology™ (the study of the unending positive purposes of the mind) are intended to help resolve individual and group suffering through empowered compassion, which is the result of marrying the Heart (kindness) and the Sword (technology).

In the field of psychology, Robert's brief therapy perspectives, models, methodologies and skills are summarized in his 15 day program for practicing therapists called *Healing The Wounded Heart: NLP as Brief Therapy*. His many seminars range from introductory courses to highly advanced work with beliefs, identity and spirituality.

As a contributor to the field of NLP, McDonald is a pioneer in the fields of psychotherapy, addictions, and co-dependence. He created *The Releasing Emotional Enmeshment Process*, the first NLP procedure to impact co-dependence and other addictions. It is featured in Steve and Connirae Andreas' *Heart of the Mind* and in John Bradshaw's *Homecoming*. He also created a variety of NLP processes which increase self-esteem, transform limiting beliefs, clarify personal boundaries, integrate various archetypes, and resolve interpersonal conflicts, e.g. Sanctuary, Self-Parenting and The Coupled Heart.

Within Psychoteleology™ he created several models and processes which build group consciousness, establish team spirit, integrate and actualize personal potentials, clarify mission, vision, and purpose, and create a context for the manifestation of genius.

Many years ago Robert, who values authenticity, humility and mercy, came to understand that his personal mission in life is to heal and be healed. His vision is to create a world filled with self-actualized individuals and groups. All of his work reflects his mission and vision and is founded on the Spiritual principle that behind every behavior, thought, feeling, fantasy, attitude and experience are universally acceptable positive purposes which often need additional modes of expression.